SOUTHERN UTE WOMEN

KATHERINE M. B. OSBURN

Southern Ute Women

AUTONOMY AND ASSIMILATION ON THE RESERVATION, 1887–1934

University of New Mexico Press Albuquerque

In memory of my mother,

Nancy Bernadette Carroll Birmingham (1930–89),

who first taught me to love history.

Library of Congress Cataloging-in-Publication Data
Osburn, Katherine

Southern Ute women : autonomy and assimilation on the reservation,
1887–1934 / Katherine M.B. Osburn, — 1st ed.

p.   cm.

Includes bibliographical references and index.

ISBN 0-8263-1862-2 (cloth). — ISBN 0-8263-1863-0 (pbk.)

1. Ute Indians — Social conditions.   2. Indian women — Southwest,
New — Social conditions.   3. Acculturation — Southwest, New.

I. Title.

E99.U8083   1998

303.48'2'0899745 — dc21   97-40742

CIP

Contents

Maps

❦

❦

Tables

Acknowledgments

Many people helped me immensely in the writing of this book. First were the excellent archivists I worked with over the years. At the Rocky Mountain Region branch of the National Archives, I would like to thank director Joel Barker, assistant director Eileen Bolger, and technicians Jim Barsi and Eric Bittner. I am especially indebted to archivist Joan Howard, also of the Rocky Mountain Region, for her willingness to locate sources in archives beyond Denver and for her helpful tips on conducting research in Washington, D.C. Joan will track records to the ends of the earth and her willingness to extend her time so generously is a great credit to the Archives. At the National Archives in Washington, D.C., I thank archivist Mary Francis Morrow and technicians Dan Law and Ira Kirschenbaum. At the Center for Southwest Studies at Fort Lewis College in Durango, Colorado, Todd Ellison and Catherine Conrad provided valuable assistance by finding records and locating photographs. Finally, I am grateful to James Muhn, land law historian for the Bureau of Land Management, who spent considerable time training me in research methodology for government records, suggested fresh approaches and sharp interpretations for the data, and greatly helped me develop a sense of professionalism as a historian.

Many people have helped me to conceptualize, sharpen, and clarify my analysis. I thank George Phillips for my original training in ethnohistorical theory and method and for reading my dissertation and offering suggestions for revisions; and David Rich Lewis for helping me construct and refine my initial questions for the dissertation prospectus and for beneficial discussions and insights on researching and writing ethnohistory. I greatly appreciate the comments of John Livingston and Joyce Goodfriend of the

University of Denver, who were on my dissertation committee. Special thanks go to Tom Altherr and Laura McCall of Metropolitan State College in Denver for their encouragement, insightful critiques, and patient assistance with my writing over the years. I would particularly like to acknowledge my original dissertation advisor J. Donald Hughes, whose criticisms were always kind and tactful, whose comments were always constructive, and who always listened carefully and prodded me to better scholarship. Most of all, to Richard O. Clemmer of the University of Denver my deepest appreciation for the many hours he spent teaching me the ethnography of the Great Basin, for his painstaking (and occasionally painful) critiques of my work over the years, and for guidance on the ethical questions of doing research on Native Americans.

My new colleagues at Tennessee Technological University have also aided me greatly in revising this manuscript for publication. Thanks go to Larry Whiteaker for beneficial comments on revising chapter 5, and to Kriste Lindenmeyer for suggesting new evaluations of my data and for assisting me with source materials and insights into the larger context of social policy and gender in the late nineteenth and early twentieth centuries. I am especially grateful to George Webb for his tremendous help, in organizing, clarifying, and strengthening the manuscript.

My colleagues in the field of Indian women's history have offered me valuable assistance and support. Carolyn Johnston of Eckerd College and Nancy Shoemaker of the University of Wisconsin, Eau Claire, have called my attention to many important issues in the scholarship of Indian women and provided much-needed encouragement and enormously helpful criticisms. I owe a special debt to Nancy Shoemaker and to Larry Durwood Ball at the University of New Mexico Press for slogging through this manuscript in dissertation form, seeing its potential as a monograph, and giving me exceptionally valuable critiques in order to shape it into this final version. I also appreciatively acknowledge copy editor Louise Cameron for her meticulous reading of the manuscript.

Finally, to my husband Charles Osburn and my daughter Jennifer Osburn my most heartfelt thanks for enduring my obsessive and sometimes psychotic behavior as I endeavored to draft a dissertation and then rework it into a publishable manuscript.

I also thank Colonial Dames of Colorado, who gave me a generous grant for my dissertation research.

Preface

During the completion of this project, the fields of women's history and Native American history have changed. That is to say that in recent years many scholars have come to believe that a truly accurate understanding of women's history is best accomplished through a gender studies approach that includes both men and women. In this new paradigm, a study of continuity and change in gender roles on the reservation would ideally focus equally on men and women. Were I beginning my research today, I would include a specific analysis comparing and contrasting how men and women responded to OIA programs. Instead, my study focuses almost exclusively on Ute women; comparisons of men's and women's lives in this period are only briefly noted. Now that scholars have begun to understand the lives of Indian women, hopefully future studies of gender and Native Americans will also consider the construction of Indian men's social roles.

In addition, the National Archives has issued new guidelines for those consulting Record Group 75, Bureau of Indian Affairs (BIA) files, designed to protect the privacy of individuals who were not public officials. These rules state that "if the records are more than 75 years old or if the subject of the record is dead then the records are open. If the records are less than 75 years old or the subject of the record is still alive" then the records are to be screened using the following guidelines:

1. All medical information is restricted wherever found.
2. Social security numbers, home addresses, and phone numbers should be restricted wherever found.
3. Any derogatory statement about an Indian that could be reasonably

considered "highly personal" should be restricted wherever found. Examples of such statements would be: "Indian is a drunk and cannot manage his affairs," "Indian is mentally incompetent and cannot be trusted to manage his affairs," "Indian is abusive and beats his wife and children," statements about sexual misconduct, etc. Statements such as "Indian cannot read," "Indian lacks business experience/sense," "Indian lacks judgment," etc. are not derogatory and are open.[1]

Following these general rules, the guidelines then explain the procedure for limiting access to such information.

National Archives staff developed these regulations in response to requests from various tribal leaders desiring to protect their people from the publication of information that they believed might cause embarrassment or shame. While most of the subjects in my study are probably dead and therefore not subject to the new restrictions, I have decided to honor the spirit of the new rules. In the sections of this book that focus on sexual "misconduct," individuals are referred to only by first names or initials. I have chosen this course of action in part because my subjects are private citizens and not public figures, and given the intensely personal nature of these discussions I feel it is appropriate to protect these people's privacy; and in part because of the larger controversy about who can best write the history of people of color.[2] While I obviously believe that this history can be written well by anyone with the appropriate training and that no one group "owns" their history, the desires of tribal leaders to shield their people from what they consider to be further exploitation cannot be taken lightly. As historians seek to look beyond tribal leaders and understand the lives of so-called "ordinary" Indian people, the potential for animosity and polarization between Indian and non-Indian scholars increases. Handling sensitive material in a manner that disregards a group's desire for personal privacy will discourage Indian peoples from working with non-Indian scholars in the future. If we are to have the fullest picture of Native American history, all scholars interested in the topic must cooperate and all voices must be heard; insensitivity does not encourage dialogue.

This decision to respect privacy means, however, that I cannot provide full references in all of my endnotes. Anyone wishing further information may contact me through this Press. I will gladly provide researchers with the appropriate file names for the original documents — providing that they agree in writing to respect these peoples' privacy. Given the history of Native and Euro-American relations, this is a small request to make.

Introduction

In 1896 David A. Day, OIA agent to the Southern Utes, remarked on how well the Utes on the reservation in southwestern Colorado were observing the Colorado game laws. He noted that they were getting along without their traditional buckskin. "As the men about all wear boots or shoes," he wrote, "and as the squaws are a secondary consideration, they do not miss the buckskin for footwear or require it for other than fancy dress." Day's comment reflected an attitude towards Native American women commonly held at the OIA, as most agents viewed women as a "secondary consideration" in matters relating to politics and economics. In one important aspect of policy, however, many OIA officials believed women had a crucial role to play on the reservation: if they could be transformed into homemakers according to the Euro-American middle-class ideal, Indian women were the potential "civilizers" of Native Americans. Thus, while women were shut out of the political and economic administration of the reservation, they were the focus of OIA programs aimed at restructuring the Indian home.[1]

Although scholars of nineteenth-century Native and Euro-American relations have examined various gender-based acculturation programs and have documented women's roles as agents of change, few works attempt a systematic study of how women in a given tribe responded to government assimilationist programs.[2] One reason for this may be the difficulty in finding information about women's lives. Government and nongovernmental agencies administered the majority of their programs on the reservation through Native American men. Women were rarely mentioned in their documents. Within the OIA, only the Home Economics and Field Matrons

Departments focused on women, and many of their records were discarded by archivists who did not appreciate their value.[3]

Nevertheless, Indian women do appear fleetingly in the historical record. Specifically, the activities of some Southern Ute women materialize in the correspondence of OIA personnel, Presbyterian missionaries' accounts, Women's Christian Temperance Union (WCTU) papers, and Colorado Federation of Women's Clubs (CFWC) documents. While these sources document Ute women's behavior, they do not include information about the women's motivations and feelings regarding their changing lives. Even letters written by Ute women and oral histories collected by researchers allow for no more than tentative conclusions, for they do not explicitly reveal individual motivation for any of the women's actions, nor do they reflect women's self-consciousness concerning culture change. Lacking specific documentation, interpretation of Ute women's hearts and minds therefore remains speculative, but anthropological information on the Utes does help illuminate possible cultural influences shaping female behavior.[4]

What do these sources tell us? Historical documents describe some women's interactions with OIA personnel, but charting the actual changes in the majority of Ute women's lives is problematic. First of all, the evidence base in this study is quite narrow. Given that very few women actually appear in the documents and that the historical record is fragmentary, it is often impossible to trace the women's ultimate fates. Were these women representative of the majority or was their behavior exceptional? To answer this question it is necessary to discover what was normative behavior for the tribe. OIA records indicate major structural changes in Ute culture, but it is unclear to what extent the Utes lived in a subculture relatively unaffected by these changes and invisible to reservation administrators. How much traditional Ute culture remained on the reservation in spite of major changes such as the imposition of Euro-American political and economic structures? Observers of the Utes in the 1930s suggested a continued Ute identity, and an investigation by the National Association of Indian Affairs, Inc. in 1935 determined:

> For thirty-five years the Southern Utes have lived on farms adjacent to white farmers. . . . They have become sedentary in their habits, have acquired property and stock, and have improved their holdings with barns, houses, fences, and corals. But in spite of this close contact with the whites . . . one has the feeling that a cultural and racial background still exists.

Anthropologists Omer C. Stewart and Marvin K. Opler, who began their fieldwork on the reservation in the early 1930s, documented both continuity and change within Ute culture.[5] It is therefore very difficult to uncover Ute norms from the official record, for much of the Utes' behavior as reported by outside observers may have represented only shallow accommodation to assimilationist demands.

Nevertheless, some generalizations can be made. All women discussed in this study sought autonomy in the face of directed culture change; the tribe as a whole also displayed this behavior. Numerous studies of colonization all over the world support the generalization that administered peoples usually found ways of opposing imposed changes or accommodating according to their own cultural norms. Therefore, while this study cannot document majority behavior with great certainty, it is reasonable to conclude that most Ute women responded to OIA programs through selective borrowing and resistance, both passive and active.[6]

This study, then, operates on two levels. On one, it documents government and nongovernmental assimilationist programs and discloses, as far as can be determined, Ute women's adaptations to them, thereby making previously invisible historical figures visible. This assessment of the interaction between Indian women and government programs asks whether Ute women reacted more conservatively to government agendas than did Ute men. On another level, this work questions how the reservation affected Ute women's social, economic, and political position, both within the tribe and within the larger context of the reservation. Here, the question of whether or not women suffered a decline in their status and power is important to an analysis of their experiences.

OIA policy sets the dates for this study. Between the years 1887 and 1934, the OIA sought to bring "civilization" to Native Americans through legislation known as the Dawes Act. OIA officials believed that Native Americans could be transformed into Christian farmers by breaking up tribal land holdings and granting individual parcels of land (known as allotments) to each family, offering vocational training (farming for men and homemaking for women), educating Indian children in government schools, and encouraging missionary activities.[7]

A significant component of this plan was restructuring of gender roles according to middle-class Euro-American ideologies of "separate spheres." In this thinking, man's primary social role was that of breadwinner while woman's was that of homemaker. Many Americans believed that the middle-class family, women's "sphere," was the cradle of "civilization." Persons concerned with "uplifting" the Indian, then, hoped to create a "civilized" home among Native Americans in which assimilated Indian women would encourage their families to adopt Euro-American customs.[8] Gender was, therefore, a crucial part of OIA policy and must be considered in a comprehensive picture of the reservation. When viewed through a lens wide enough to include gender, the reservation takes on a complex configuration.

First, the patriarchal structure of the reservation becomes apparent. Under OIA political organization the Utes were an administered people. Office personnel, both on and off the reservation, made the major political decisions for the Utes. Ute men had very little say in the implementation of governmental policies but Ute women were completely shut out. When it came time for treaties, councils, or economic interactions with the tribes, OIA officials addressed Indian men. In the late nineteenth and early twentieth centuries, Indian reservations were organized around the same sexist principles that governed the larger United States society; that is, women were excluded from political decision making and full economic participation.

But the creation of a patriarchal reservation system (in contrast to a traditionally egalitarian Ute culture) is only part of the story; official policy was not necessarily the defining characteristic of the reservation experience. Ute women's activities, often barely visible in the records and generally overlooked by historians, provide a fuller account of reservation life. Some Ute women, accustomed to sharing in public decision making before the reservation, forced their way into the political process on numerous occasions. They participated in councils and public debates on all aspects of reservation policy, they wrote letters and petitions demanding redress of their grievances, and they led resistance to off-reservation schooling for their children. They attempted, with limited success, to carve out for themselves a place of autonomy in the new political order.

The reservation's economic structure was also patriarchal. Expecting them to be economically dependent on men, agents denied women a significant role in the reservation economy. Men received the training and incentives to be producers, while women were given instruction in homemaking. The OIA considered husbands (unless they were hopeless ne'er-do-wells) to be the heads of families and gave them control of the finances, preferring that they sign the receipts for rations and annuity monies (small sums of money given to tribal members for land sales and oil or gas leases) on behalf of their families. In the first generation of allottees, wives were excluded from property ownership, leaving them without property in cases of divorce.

As in the area of politics, however, many Ute women resisted these plans and found ways to participate in the reservation economy. They did wage work, made and sold craft items, leased and sold their lands, ran farms and reared livestock, gathered and processed wild foods, and contributed their share of annuity monies to their households. Women's material contributions were critical to the tribe's survival. Over the protests of agents, women insisted on actively participating in the granting of rations, and several women also attempted to secure rights to family property in divorce settlements. Here, most women repudiated Euro-American gender roles by refusing to be shut out of the productive realm.

The most concentrated assault on gender roles came in the OIA attempts to change the family. Office personnel believed that the allotment would form the basis for a nuclear family in which Indian women would create a private "sphere" of domesticity — a "civilized" home to lead their families into Euro-American ways. To "lift" Native American women to this level, the OIA sent special workers, called field matrons, into Indian homes to remake them according to Euro-American standards of cleanliness, subsistence tasks, and aesthetics, and to train Indian women in the "proper" gender behavior.

Ute women responded to the field matrons with a combination of selective borrowing and passive resistance. Initially, they hindered attempts to make them into "homemakers" by refusing to move into permanent houses. They also continued their customary patterns of living in extended families, challenging the concept of the nuclear family that underpinned the matrons' family ideal. Ute women participated only selectively in many matrons' programs. A number of them attended cooking and sewing classes but, despite OIA censure, continued their established practice of communal work. Some of them participated in the matrons' homemaking contests and made exhibits for Ute fairs. These actions, however, may have been motivated by the free food and clothing that the matron provided to prepare for the event or by the prize money offered, rather than by a desire to celebrate Euro-American homemaking techniques. The matrons' greatest impact was in health care. Numerous women came to the matrons for medicine and prenatal care and began to have their children in hospitals. There is also some evidence that many were receptive to matrons' ideas about housekeeping and sanitation practices, and most women enthusiastically embraced labor-saving technology for the home.

Finally, OIA agents intruded into Ute sexual behavior. Because the Utes tolerated sex outside of marriage, married without legal proceedings, occasionally practiced polygamy, and allowed for easy divorce, the OIA considered them immoral. Through a combination of exhortation and sanctions, agents promoted Euro-American ideals of premarital chastity and permanent, legal, monogamous marriages. OIA personnel attempted to use women as the primary agents of change in the area of morals. To this end, one agent tried to coerce women into lawful marriages by threatening their children's inheritances. Others tried to force women who were pregnant out of wedlock to marry, sought to return "runaway" wives to their husbands, and annulled unions they deemed unsatisfactory. In carrying out this agenda, male agents sometimes exhibited a double standard, punishing women's transgressions against the official moral code while overlooking men's.

A number of Ute women (and men) seem to have resisted coercion in their sexual and marital behavior. While the number of legal marriages rose during this time (some OIA agents credited the influence of women), evidence from anthropological fieldwork of the late 1920s and early 1930s suggests that many Utes may not have kept these contracts, preferring instead to practice serial monogamy behind the agents' backs. Among a group of unmarried pregnant women, all but one refused to marry their babies' fathers, and the "runaway" wives who appear in these records rarely returned. In short, Ute women were no more willing to surrender personal autonomy than they were to refrain from political and economic participation.

To assume, then, that all Ute women were entirely subjugated because OIA policy created a sexist society on the reservation is to give altogether too much weight to the activities of OIA administrators. Inasmuch as women's activities can be uncovered, they suggest that women pursued their own agendas for cooperation with or resistance to OIA policies, and that a distinctly Ute identity continued on the reservation throughout the period of forced assimilation. Finally, there is no evidence that any Ute women during this era internalized the OIA's doctrine of female subordination to men, or that most Ute men attempted to dominate Ute women.

Women's behavior was frequently in direct opposition to OIA plans to restructure Native American gender roles. However, an interpretation of women's conduct must be cautious. Ute women's activities may have been motivated less by a wish to resist patriarchy and more by a desire to withstand domination by the United States government. Some strategies might have been responses to reservation poverty rather than refusals of assimilationist demands. In short, women's actions may have resulted in resistance to patriarchal gender roles when they were not necessarily originally intended as such.

Many of the issues women raised with the OIA hierarchy — land policies, tribal finances, and educational matters — were important to the tribe as a whole and were also topics that men addressed. Some women added their voices to men's in speaking for tribal autonomy. Other women wrote more personal letters to the OIA, protesting their individual treatment by OIA personnel. While these women sought personal autonomy, they may not have been speaking as women disputing men but as Utes opposing "outside" interference in their private affairs. Likewise, although women's financial contributions to their families contradicted OIA plans to make them dependent on their husbands, women probably viewed their activities as economic survival, not resistance to female dependency. Overall, women's actions may not have been motivated by a conscious opposition to alien gender roles but by hostility to alien control in general.[9]

In analyzing the responses of Ute women to OIA policy, it becomes apparent that men and women often reacted in very similar ways. While other historians have found Indian women's reactions to assimilationist efforts to be far more conservative than men's, this does not seem to be the case among the Utes. Although women were sometimes at the forefront of certain areas of resistance, both sexes on the Southern Ute reservation interacted with the OIA as native peoples under a colonial regime. Their activities were part of an overall attempt by the tribe to retain as much autonomy as was possible under forced culture change. In this, women's behavior was as important as men's and deserves to be recovered from the historical record.[10]

Those who desired to "uplift" the Indians dreamed of a community of prosperous farmers and dependent farm wives with families structured on the middle-class Euro-American ideals of privatism and domesticity; this vision never crystallized on the Southern Ute reservation. The failure of assimilationist policies was partially due to a lack of funds for farming programs. Impersonal economic forces also played a role, for market conditions in southern Colorado weakened the viability of commercial farming for small land owners, and struggles over water rights hindered the development of many Indian farms. The activities of Native Americans in both resisting and selectively adopting items from the OIA agenda, however, also contributed to the outcome of government policy. On the Southern Ute reservation, in the late nineteenth and early twentieth centuries, women played a significant role in this process.

ONE

The People of the Shining Mountains

According to sixteenth-century Spanish documents, the Ute Indians oc-cupied considerable territory in the Rocky Mountains and Great Basin at the time of contact. Their range extended from the Oquirrh Mountains in the west, the Uintah Mountains and Yampa River in the north, the Front Range of the Rockies in the east, and the San Juan River in the south. Scholars are uncertain as to exactly when and how they came to inhabit this area. After their initial migration across the Bering Strait, the ancestors of the Utes either came across the deserts of the Great Basin and spread eastward into the Rockies, or they migrated down the eastern front of the Rocky Mountains and moved west into the Great Basin.[1]

Before confinement to a reservation, the Utes hunted, fished, and gath-ered and processed seeds, roots, tubers, berries, thistles, and cactus blos-soms. They moved in seasonal migrations, hunting and gathering in the mountains from early spring until late summer and then moving to lower elevations for the winter. Hunting and foraging parties, consisting of small groupings of bilateral extended families, tended to stay within the same regions. Because they traveled in a given area, these groups were identified as territorial bands.[2]

The seven Ute bands and their territories were as follows: the Mouache, in southern Colorado and northern New Mexico; the Capote, in the San Luis Valley and north-central New Mexico; the Weminuche, in the San Juan River valley and northwestern New Mexico; the Tabegauche (or Un-compahgre) in the valleys of the Gunnison and Uncompahgre Rivers in Colorado; the Grand River and Yampa River bands, named after the rivers; and the Uintah Utes in the Uintah Basin in northwest Colorado and north-eastern Utah. The southernmost bands—the Capote, Mouache and We-minuche—were known as the Southern Utes. All the Utes in Colorado, New Mexico, and Utah numbered about 8,000 at the time of contact.[3]

The Utes acquired horses at some point in the mid-seventeenth century. Several bands then moved out onto the Plains and hunted buffalo—their new economic mainstay—which provided tepees, clothing, blankets, and horn implements. Buffalo meat provided a secure food supply so that families could gather into larger bands. Ute parents also occasionally bartered their children as slaves to the Spanish in exchange for horses, perhaps reasoning that without horses they would be unable to protect themselves from other mounted tribes. As the slave trade grew, the Utes began stealing children from sedentary groups, such as the Paiutes, and selling them to obtain horses.[4]

During the eighteenth century, the Southern Utes expanded their territory through raiding and trade affiliations. According to the needs of the moment, they pursued a pattern of shifting alliances and raids between the Comanches (who moved into the region around the beginning of the eighteenth century), the Kiowas, the Arapahos, the Cheyennes, the Apaches, the Pueblos, and Spanish settlers. Intense warfare alternated with periods of peace, during which time the Utes traded with all of the above listed groups at Taos, New Mexico. The Utes exchanged tanned hides, furs, fresh meat, baskets, and slaves for textiles, produce, metal goods, turquoise, pottery, and horses.[5]

Because of increasing trade during the nineteenth century, more people moved into Ute territory. In the 1820s and 1830s trade flourished between Americans at Bent's Fort (on the Arkansas River in southeastern Colorado) and Mexicans at Santa Fe. The Mexican government gave presents to the Utes to ensure peaceful travel through their territory to these markets. In the late 1830s Mexican cowboys bringing cattle herds entered the region. The Utes interacted extensively with these new settlers, forming friendships and sexual liaisons and occasionally trading children to the ranchers for horses. Conflict sometimes occurred when Hispanic herds encroached on Ute lands and drove out game. The Indians then retaliated by sporadic raids on settlements. Until the American government took control of this territory under the treaty of Guadalupe-Hidalgo in 1848, the Utes and their neighbors were alternatively allies and enemies. The American period marked the end of Ute expansion and autonomy.[6]

When the Utes came under the authority of the United States government, in 1848, Euro-American settlers were flooding west onto Indian

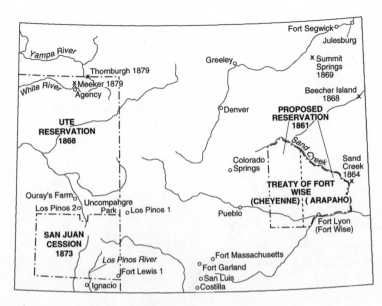

MAP 1. UTE RESERVATIONS, 1848–1879.

land, rousing conflict over resources. In response, government officials established and garrisoned forts in the West. At the same time, the OIA acted to relocate Western tribes on reservations, where they could be taught farming and "civilized" pursuits.[7] The government pursued this reservation policy with the Utes.

Beginning in 1849, the United States government signed a series of treaties with the Utes, creating and — as conflict occurred between Utes and settlers — continually redefining a reservation for them. In 1868 the Great Ute Treaty outlined a reservation containing about a fourth of Colorado Territory, from the White River in the north to New Mexico in the south, and from the Utah border in the west to the present town of Gunnison in the east. Because of the size of the reservation, the treaty established two agencies: one in the north and one in the south. In 1873, under the Brunot Agreement, the Utes surrendered 6,000 square miles of their land (about a quarter of the reservation) to the United States in return for $25,000 annually "forever."[8]

Anglo-Americans in Colorado had mixed feelings about the Utes' presence. Many settlers near the agencies pressured government officials to transfer the Indians to Utah; others, however, lobbied against Ute removal.

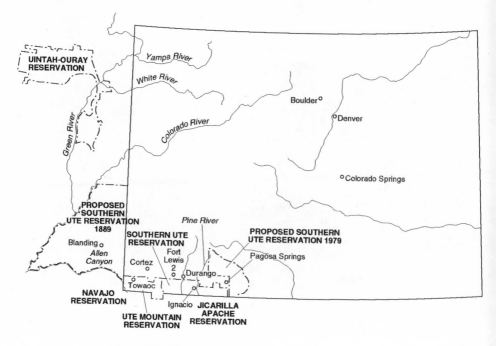

MAP 2. UTE RESERVATIONS, 1880–1979.

A coalition of Utah citizens (who did not want "savage" Indians in their midst) and "Friends of the Indians" — including OIA employees, church groups, and professional educators (who feared that the Utes would not assimilate if allowed to flee into Utah) — wanted the Utes to remain in Colorado and take up farming along the La Plata River. In 1880, Congress drafted an agreement implementing this idea, which Ute leaders signed. Persons in favor of removal, however, opposed the 1880 agreement and every year thereafter introduced removal bills into Congress. To their dismay, they failed at every attempt.[9]

While the removal debate raged, reformers concerned with assimilating the Indians concluded that reservations, with their communal land base and isolation from "civilized" Americans, kept tribal identity alive and hindered assimilation. Reservations, they argued, must be dismantled and the Indians given individual plots of land. In 1887 men and women committed to this policy drafted legislation known as the General Allotment or Dawes Act. The act emphasized four concepts: allotment of lands in severalty to individual Indians, vocational training for adults (farming for Indian men and homemaking for Indian women), education in "civilized" ways at government schools for Indian children, and involvement of churches — both in policy making and in missionary work among allotted tribes.[10]

The Dawes Act granted allotments of 160 acres to heads of families and single people over the age of eighteen. Orphans under the age of eighteen and other single people under eighteen received forty acres. The United States government held the allotments in trust for twenty-five years (or longer if the agent deemed it necessary) so that the owners could not sell the land or be taxed on it. Once the Indians had selected allotments, the act provided that the "surplus" lands be opened for purchase by non-Indians. Some policy makers felt that this legislation provided the perfect solution to the removal controversy: it would force the Indians to acculturate, keep them out of Utah, and allow Coloradoans who favored removal to get their hands on Ute lands. Commissioner of Indian Affairs (CIA) Thomas Jefferson Morgan finally settled the removal question in 1890 by ruling that the Utes must remain in Colorado and begin this latest phase of assimilationist policy.[11]

The Utes were divided over the question of removal. Agents' monthly reports for the year 1890 speak of tremendous upheaval on the reservation over the issue. Chief Ignacio of the Weminuche band and Buckskin Charley of the Mouache band favored removal. They traveled to Washington in 1886 where they requested permission from the Senate Committee on Indian Affairs to relocate in Utah. Their followers refused to farm or send their children to school, and sometimes they stormed the agent's office demanding to be sent to Utah. Other Utes resisted relocation, and one quarrel over the issue ended in a knife fight. The Indians held large council meetings vehemently debating the issue, but regardless of Ute opinion the OIA continued with its assimilationist plans.[12]

In 1895 Congress passed the Hunter Act implementing the Dawes plan on the Southern Ute reservation. The act stated that Indians who did not desire to be allotted could settle on the western end of the reservation (along the extreme southwestern border of Colorado) and hold land communally. The Weminuche band took advantage of this provision and claimed the land that came to be known as the Ute Mountain reservation. In 1897 the OIA opened the Navajo Springs agency, near Cortez, Colorado, to administer the unallotted Weminuche. The Capote and Mouache bands agreed to take allotments, and the OIA administered them through the Southern Ute agency. After the Indians had chosen their farms, Hispanic and Anglo settlers gradually moved onto what had been Ute lands. Although the reservation was dissolved as a geographic entity, it still remained as two administrative units — Ute Mountain and Southern Ute.[13]

The Southern Ute agency was the scene of the United States government's campaign to assimilate the Utes, and OIA involvement in every detail of Ute lives was constant, long-term, and relatively well documented. The OIA was not alone in its mission, however. Other organizations also attempted to "uplift" the Utes from their "savage" state. Presbyterian missionaries and clubwomen representing both the Women's Christian Temperance Union (WCTU) and the Colorado Federation of Women's Clubs (CFWC) contributed to the efforts to transform Ute culture.[14]

The OIA supported missionary activity through land grants and contracts for educational services. In 1894 Presbyterian minister Antonio Jose Anastacio Rodriguez petitioned the secretary of the interior for church land on the reservation. Emmanuel Presbyterian Church opened in Ignacio a year later. A Women's Home Mission group in the East contributed to the church's support until, in 1901, the congregation could support itself.[15]

Ute agents were initially skeptical of the Presbyterians' chances for success because most Utes who embraced Christianity were Catholic, having adopted Catholicism from nearby Hispanics. The OIA encouraged these conversions by granting Father Francis A. Munoz three acres of land near the agency for a church, in 1903. In 1906 the OIA gave ten acres to Father F. B. Gomez to build a school, and in 1910 the church got two more acres for a cemetery. So many Utes were involved with Catholic activities that, in 1913, Agent Stephen Abbot told his supplier of beef to deliver his shipment before a Catholic Church fiesta because the majority of Indians would be attending the festivities the following day.[16]

True to the agents' predictions, Emmanuel Presbyterian Church never drew large numbers of Utes. By 1902 only thirty-eight Utes attended, and converts were often harassed by the other Indians. Women apparently played a role in the initial resistance to the mission. Rodriguez reported, "For a long time no women could be induced to come, but at length a few of these, too, began to attend and show a little interest." That "interest" eventually led some women to embrace Presbyterianism. In 1902 Rodriguez's assistant, Miss Elizabeth McAllister, attended weddings of these converts. She wrote, "three couples had the marriage ceremony performed legally. They were people who had lived together for years." She also commented that the Christian Indian women's homes were "much better" than their unconverted neighbors and their husbands farmed and did wage work on the local irrigation ditches and in the nearby coal mines.[17]

Among the allotted Utes, then, Presbyterianism had a limited appeal, but a second mission at Ute Mountain had practically none. In 1897 Miss Floretta Shields opened — at her own expense — a mission and school in Cortez, Colorado, among the unallotted Weminuche band. The Presbyterian Women's Home Mission Board took over its sponsorship shortly after the mission opened. Shields conducted Sunday-school services in her home during the morning, and in the afternoon she visited tepees "to talk and pray, and hold services of song." In her missionary reports, Shields lamented that her work was slowed for want of an interpreter.[18]

Rather than attempting to convert influential headmen, as the other Presbyterian mission did, Shields approached the Utes through women's concerns. She nursed the sick, opened a school for the children, and attempted to train Ute women in Anglo-American homemaking skills. The women's first reaction to her was one of hostility, but she gradually made friends with several young wives who then attended some of her homemaking classes. She claimed to have had twenty-five children at her school by 1906. The Weminuches' nomadic subsistence base limited Shields' contact with the Indians and there are no records of any conversions under her ministry. She left the mission in early 1906 because of ill health. The mission stayed open but was never successful.[19]

The few Presbyterian Utes resided at Ignacio. Those who converted may have done so out of sincere religious convictions, but it is more likely that they had a variety of motives. Mrs. Rodriguez nursed the sick, perhaps drawing some into association with the church. Although mission records do not reveal the extent of its charitable work, perhaps ministers and their assistants offered food and clothing as an incentive to neophytes.[20] Assimilation, however, seems to have played a significant role in conversions.

Presbyterian converts were among the more acculturated Utes who farmed, sent their children to school, and held appointments to the tribal council and police. The star disciples of the mission were Julian Buck, son of Mouache chief Buckskin Charley, and Severo, chief of the Capote band. Julian Buck had been educated in the Albuquerque Indian school and converted in 1897 while working as Rodriguez's translator. Severo was not educated but reservation officials frequently praised him "for he always [gave] a good example to the rest of the Indians." The rest of the Presbyterian converts were close friends and family of these influential leaders. These Utes may have sensed that Protestantism was more acceptable than Catholicism to reservation officials. The missionary school could also have been a draw for these Utes, for there was no government school on the reservation at the time. Since attendance figures for the school are missing, it is impossible to say how many Ute children attended. Floretta Shields, as previously mentioned, claimed to have had many Ute students in her school.[21]

Along with representing the Presbyterians on the reservation, Shields also represented the WCTU. She began in 1901 as department chair for the Fifteenth District of the Colorado WCTU. In 1903 the State Executive Committee of the WCTU decided to take up "Work Among the Indians." Shields served as state superintendent for Indian work in 1904–5.[22] In 1904 Shields founded a Ladies' Temperance Legion (LTL) on the reservation and sent WCTU publications *The Union Signal* and *The Crusader* to Indian schools at Ignacio and Fort Lewis. In 1905 she sponsored a traveling WCTU presentation (which included a stereopticon show, "Ten Nights in a Bar-room") at the Fort Lewis and Southern Ute boarding schools. Her only successes were in recruiting more female OIA employees for LTL. Three women continued the WCTU after Shields left, but they failed to halt Indian drinking.[23]

The WCTU had nothing to give the Utes beyond literature (which the Utes could not read) and white ribbon badges (which they apparently did not want). WCTU notions on the evils of drink, as presented in "Ten Nights in a Bar-room," were totally bound-up in Euro-American culture and were probably incomprehensible to most Utes.[24] Finally, judging by their complete lack of interest in joining the LTL, Ute women completely rejected the role of moral guardian that the WCTU preached.

The final nongovernment agency to work at Southern Ute was the CFWC. Founded in 1895 as an umbrella group for Colorado women's clubs, the Federation created a Division of Indian Welfare in 1925. The clubwomen's activities included the study of Indian artifacts, art, literature, and music. The CFWC also lobbied for legislation on both the state and national levels, and their agenda mirrored the OIA's in its emphasis on education and indoctrination in Euro-American culture. Clubwomen raised money to improve reservation schools and to develop "an independent and self-sustaining American citizenship" among Indians.[25]

While the CFWC was similar to the OIA in some of its ethnocentric paternalistic programs, it also became a force for genuine activism and appreciation for native culture. The Colorado Federation's chairman for Indian Welfare, Mrs. Charles W. Wiegel (Nellie), was a tireless crusader for Ute causes. Appointed in 1926, Wiegel immediately selected a committee to investigate conditions at Southern Ute, established a State Commission on Indian Welfare in the Governor's office (Colorado governor William H. Adams immediately appointed her chair), and introduced a bill to erect a memorial to Ute chief Ouray in Montrose, Colorado.[26]

Over her twenty-year career as an Indian activist, Wiegel also responded to individual appeals of many Utes. Seeking redress for their personal grievances, Wiegel wrote angry letters to OIA personnel on behalf of "her" Utes (as she called them). She attempted to protect oil and water resources and annuities, she called on the government to honor treaty obligations, and she sought to get Ute children admitted to public schools near the reservation. She also demanded that the OIA account for Ute funds. Time and again, OIA officials thanked Wiegel for her interest, but suggested she undertake projects for Ute women and children instead.[27]

While Wiegel started a "special club among the young women of [the] reservation to bring before them ideals of better home life," she did not confine herself to "women's" projects. Rather, she continually involved herself in every aspect of reservation administration — especially financial matters.[28] Wiegel's activism blended a paternalistic concern for acculturating the Utes with a genuine respect for certain aspects of their culture. She told the *Rocky Mountain News:*

> We should teach them [the Utes] to be proud of their Indian blood, proud of their heritage of bravery. It is a mistake to try to make whites of them.

"Her Utes" were "noble savages" who needed help adjusting to modernity. Initially she viewed herself as a facilitator in that process, but gradually she became an activist, challenging the United States government on behalf of the Ute people.[29]

As Wiegel continued to agitate for Ute causes, however, many bureaucrats grew hostile toward her. In 1927 OIA investigator H. H. Fiske called her "difficult, demanding, [and] a gabster, spreading her secrets wherever she thinks she may find a retentive ear." Her final fall from grace came when she accused Agent Edward Peacore of fraud and sexual misconduct. The ensuing investigation lasted from 1931 to 1933 and was intensely acrimonious. As a result of the investigation, Wiegel was, for a time, completely discredited. In 1932 CIA Charles J. Rhodes sent her a letter stating that her participation in Indian affairs was no longer welcomed. Wiegel was forced out of her position as Chairman of Indian Welfare in the CFWC in 1932, and the Colorado State Indian Commission was abolished in January of 1933. Wiegel responded by charging that she had been unjustly thrust out of Indian affairs in Colorado.[30]

No Utes left any specific comments on Wiegel's programs. According to CFWC records, however, the tribe seemed to appreciate her efforts to help.

Many Utes called on Wiegel to aid them with personal issues concerning
schooling or tribal finances, and the tribe adopted her as a "Red Sister." In
the midst of the controversy over Peacore, in 1932, Mouache leader Buckskin Charley spoke on her behalf at the thirty-eighth annual CFWC convention in Durango, Colorado.[31]

The effectiveness of Wiegel's activities is difficult to gauge, but her presence on the reservation provided the Utes with a means to challenge the
authority of the OIA. Many Utes perceived Wiegel as powerful. The huge
fracas her investigations stirred up — OIA inspectors, delegations of towns-
people, and committees of clubwomen descending on the reservation —
reinforced this perception. To have such a woman acting as their advocate
probably gave some Utes a sense of control in situations where they would
otherwise have felt helpless.

Conclusions

After centuries of political autonomy and military dominance over a wide
range of territory, the Utes were confined to reservations in Colorado and
Utah and brought under the administration of the OIA. The OIA subse-
quently divided the Colorado tribe into two administrative units — the unallotted Weminuche band on the western half of the reservation, and the
allotted Capote and Mouache bands on the eastern half. On the allotted
portion of the reservation, known as Southern Ute, the OIA initiated a
crusade to assimilate the Indians, which lasted from 1895 when the allotment process was instituted to 1934 when the government shifted its policy
away from forced culture change.

Nongovernmental organizations also worked to reinforce OIA assimilationist goals at Southern Ute. Their effectiveness, however, appears to have
been minimal. Each of these associations could promote its programs, but
the Utes could choose not to participate, for the organizations had no
coercive power. Only the OIA could bring sanctions against the Utes for
noncooperation. This meant that the other groups had to offer something
attractive enough to win the Utes' participation.

The Indians viewed these organizations from the perspective of their
own agendas. There is no evidence that they desired to embrace the Euro-
American cultural goals being propagated. Rather, the Utes' interaction
with nongovernmental agencies was based on their perceptions of how
a particular group could assist them with economic and cultural issues.

Whenever possible, the Utes used the groups as a method of resisting the OIA program.

Assimilationist policies of governmental and nongovernmental agencies focused in part on gender roles. Policy was both implicit—shutting Ute women out of political activities and promoting economic dependency on men—and explicit—attempting to change the way Ute women constructed their roles of wife and mother. The Utes responded to these programs with shifting patterns of cooperation and resistance.

TWO

Women and Public Leadership

Nowhere in its official policy did the OIA state that Native American women would be excluded from political leadership on the reservation. No Southern Ute agent ever officially declared that all policy decisions would be made by agents and Indian men. Rather, agents simply ignored women when they called councils or when they brought "chiefs and headmen" to Washington to discuss tribal matters. On the reservation, Ute men were the official tribal representatives for all areas of public policy. Indian men negotiated the establishment of the reservation, met in councils to debate removal, approved the provisions of the Hunter Act granting the Utes allotments, and met in all-male councils to establish education procedures.[1] Once policy decisions had been made, agents implemented them through men, whom they viewed as the heads of households, representing their families to reservation officials. The OIA expected a level of male leadership between the home and reservation political structure.[2] Implicitly, OIA officials assumed Ute women's roles to be private, rather than public, and secondary to men's.

Many Ute women, however, did not accept this passive role. Much to the irritation of agents, Ute women intruded into the public sphere. They sought to protect their interests in annuities and allotments and joined with men in public forums to criticize OIA policy. Women were active in the struggle over education, helping to decide which schools their children would attend. In several areas of policy implementation, women led resistance to OIA plans. Their refusal to send their children to unsafe schools forced the OIA to modify the Utes' educational facilities. Women also provided public leadership among the Utes in nativistic movements and were an important part of resistance to sedentism. An examination of the implementation of OIA policy reveals women's refusal to be excluded from a public role. Their behavior represented a continuation of the traditional Ute public roles for women.

In aboriginal times, the Utes had no formal political organizations with coercive power. Men, therefore, had no political basis for dominance over women. Moreover, since the family constituted the primary economic and political structures, the Euro-American distinction between public and private roles was meaningless. In the Ute kinship system gender roles were egalitarian, for age, rather than sex, was the primary basis for influence. Elders could not order a family member to do something, but families valued their guidance. Older relatives presided over family rituals such as rites of passage at birth and puberty. In cases of interpersonal disputes, the aggrieved party could appeal to the older relatives of the alleged perpetrator or take his or her grievance directly to the individual.[3] Subsistence tasks and defensive warfare were organized around extended families. Respected elders, male or female, guided these collective activities.

Before the introduction of the horse, the Utes rarely raided other Indians. Afterwards, however, they fought over resources and territory with the Plains Indians to the east and the Navajos to the south. Men generally led these raids, though women could as well.[4] As Utes struck the surrounding peoples for horses and slaves, they organized into larger bands around successful male warriors. Following the traditional Ute patterns of leadership, these men had no coercive power, and their influence lasted only as long as they were successful in raiding and generous with their plunder. Band leadership did not replace the authority of family elders but rather supplemented it, adding a new category of communal task to the activities of the family. While men led bands, women still had a voice in group decisions, for leaders had to have public support. Women's opinions concerning group activities were given equal weight with men's. Men and women were free to leave the band at any time, should they feel their interests were not properly represented.[5]

The changes engendered by the horse affected women's lives in important ways. Warfare provided women with new means to achieve status. While their men were away on raids, women guarded the camp belongings, ready to flee enemy raiders should any retaliate, and when battles occurred in Ute territory, women armed themselves and followed the men into battle to scalp and gather loot. The redistribution of booty in victory ceremonies brought these women honor and prestige. They even had a women's auxiliary warrior sodality with their own songs and a victory dance, done with a lame step to symbolize a heavy load of spoils.[6]

Women's victory dances reflected their place in Ute religion, another area for public influence. Religion, a source of sexual inequality in some cultures, was egalitarian in Ute culture. The Utes believed that supernatural power infused the entire universe. This power was both male and female, and interaction between these two forces was the source of creation. The supreme power was the Creator, who was identified with the sun, or with Sunawavi, the Wolf (also called Shin-au-vi), a culture-hero and trickster. While the Utes viewed this god as male, they did not believe that he alone created humanity. Rather, he had sex with a woman who then gave birth to the human race. In Ute myth, Water Grandmother created the land from her body when the world consisted only of the ocean. Other natural elements had supernatural power, including the moon and stars, lightning and wind, and eagles, elks, antelope, and buffalo. The Utes believed some of these phenomena were female.[7]

Supernatural power could come to men and women in dreams. Men and women, then, could become shamans and exercise influence beyond their immediate families. Women probably did not hold this position until after menopause, however, for the Utes believed that women's menstrual blood was a dangerous spiritual force. At her first menstruation, a young woman was isolated from the camp, and her grandmother (or older female relative) instructed her to separate herself during each successive period, lest her blood cause illness to men. If she ate fish or meat at this time, she could spoil the hunting or fishing abilities of her male relatives. According to the Utes, women who did not obey these rules rapidly became old and crippled. By separating menstruating women from the group the Utes acknowledged women's ability to give life and awarded them respect and status.[8]

In short, before confinement to the reservation, the Utes recognized significant differences in gender roles but did not value one gender more highly than the other. Women were equal members of their families and bands. They did not restrict their activities to the home and allow men to rule in the public realm. Rather, they participated in councils, were active in warfare, and provided leadership and power in spiritual matters. After relocation to the reservation, women continued to insist on participation in public affairs.

Women and Policy Councils

Allotments and Finances

Not recognizing women's important position in decision making, OIA personnel negotiated all land issues with Ute men. Beginning with the Great

Ute Treaty of 1868, which established the reservation, agents called councils of Ute men. In 1886, 1890, and 1894 agents met with "most of the chiefs and headmen" to discuss moving the three bands to Utah. Once the removal issue was settled in favor of the Utes remaining in Colorado, the tribe met to choose whether to be allotted lands in severalty. Allotment was to "take effect only upon the acceptance thereof and consent thereto by a majority of all the male adult Indians at Southern Ute." CIA Daniel M. Browning instructed Meredith Kidd of the Southern Ute Allotment Commission to obtain the consent of the male Indians — Agent David A. Day would convene the men and provide an interpreter.[9] Ute and Anglo men, then, made all the official decisions regarding apportionments of land on the reservation.

Although they were excluded from the councils that debated acceptance of the Hunter Act, women made sure their concerns entered into the deliberations. Undoubtedly at the request of the women, Ute men prodded allotment commissioner Kidd to write to Washington for assurances that women and children would not lose their annuities if the tribe accepted allotments. CIA Browning instructed Kidd to convince the Indians that the government would continue to provide annuities for all the Utes after they received their land.[10] Thus, before the allotment process began, women saw that their interests were represented.

Agent David F. Day, who was in charge of Southern Utes at the time of allotments in 1895, reported that the women apparently overcame their reticence about accepting land:

> The effect of allotment is gratifying, as pride of ownership seems to have actuated the able-bodied — even the squaws — in getting out posts and preparing to fence a part of their holdings. They are interested in seeing each and every corner and are anxious as to wagons, wire, and implements.[11]

Agent Day interpreted the flurry of activity as a sign that Ute women were excited about the idea of private property, but Ute actions were actually animated by fear that their holdings were not secure. Special Agent G. B. Perry, who came to the reservation in 1899 to observe the effects of allotment, noted that many Utes expressed apprehension over Anglos moving onto the reservation. To avoid "serious trouble," they demanded that he help them fence their lands.[12] Ute women fenced their allotments, then, to safeguard their property rather than to express "pride of ownership." Despite their official exclusion from the allotment process, Ute women actively sought to protect their interests.

Women also participated eagerly in public forums about reservation policy. The Indians themselves, not the agents, initiated these gatherings, and they were conducted according to Ute gender roles. In August of 1890, Agent Charles A. Bartholomew noted:

> Partially owing to a cartoon which appeared in a neighboring paper there was held this day the biggest council of chiefs and headmen ever remembered at this agency . . . [the Utes] discussed the question [of removal] vehemently, the squaws taking part and neglecting their homes to come.[13]

"Squaws," along with several men, also confronted Agent Bartholomew in 1891, expressing suspicion as to the cause of a flu epidemic that had claimed many lives on the reservation. The Utes blamed witchcraft, and Bartholomew feared they suspected that he was the witch; he managed, after several attempts, to convince them of his innocence.[14]

Women were active in councils that met to discuss tribal finances. In 1896, 150 women attended a council initiated by the Utes to claim monies promised them by the government. The group passed a resolution and elected three delegates (all male) to travel to Washington to present their case to the OIA. In 1911 Agent Charles Werner reported that the Utes were "very indignant and have held three councils" demanding control of their annuity monies. Their protests continued through 1912 and 1913; some Utes hired lawyers who contacted congressmen, while men and women refused to work their farms until their payments and rations were distributed. In 1916, 1919, 1921, 1925, and 1926 councils of men and women petitioned Washington for annuities, supplies, and rations "as called for by treaty obligations."[15]

One woman in particular, Mary Baker Pena, was especially vocal. Mary signed several group petitions but she also wrote to the commissioner herself in 1925, filing her own complaints against Agent Edward E. McKean. She accused him of not allowing her to spend her own money, failing to fix her roof, refusing to make a man with a stable on her property pay rent, withholding funds received from the sale of some of her land to the Denver–Rio Grande Railroad, and telling local merchants not to trust the Utes. "The utes [sic] are the poorest people on earth," she concluded; "to save us from starving we will have to mortgage our only property. . . . O Commissioner you don't know what he is doing with us."[16]

The OIA responded by sending Special Inspector T. B. Roberts to the reservation. Roberts spoke with agency employees, including McKean, and concluded Mary's charges were groundless. He agreed with McKean's assessment that she was "ungrateful." The commissioner then wrote to Mary, dismissing her concerns. Mary received no satisfaction for her complaints, but her letter is an important example of how some Ute women acted through political channels to redress their grievances.[17] Refusing to be passive, at least one woman directly challenged reservation authorities.

Education

Similarly, many women disputed reservation policy on educational matters. Agents called councils with men to recruit Ute children for OIA schools; in the late nineteenth century these were generally boarding schools. In 1880 Agent Henry Page promised the Indian Office that he could "induce some of the most peaceable and intelligent men to consent to allow their children to be taken to Carlisle [Indian school]." After promising the Utes that several parents could accompany their children to school, Page informed the CIA that fifteen or twenty pupils were ready to go. In 1881, however, when he arranged for the students to leave, a group of men and women demanded to know how many parents could make the trip. When Page could not give them a specific reply, the Utes declared that their children would remain at home.[18]

Frustrated, the next agent shifted tactics. In 1883, after a council meeting during which Weminuche chief Ignacio "bitterly opposed" his requests for children, Agent Warren Patten offered Ignacio a $200 bribe to relinquish his children for schooling. Secretary of the Interior Henry M. Teller approved of Patten's plan and authorized the expenditure. Patten distributed the money and Ignacio surrendered his band's children. The OIA also gave the men tools, implements, and jobs on the police force as rewards for sending their children to school.[19] OIA correspondence does not indicate how the women of Ignacio's band responded to these practices. Nevertheless, it is difficult to imagine that they would allow their children to be taken without their consent. They were undoubtedly involved in the decision to send the children, yet they were not consulted nor did they receive any rewards for their cooperation.

In keeping with the custom of male delegations, it was men that agents took when placing or visiting children in off-reservation boarding schools. Warren Patten and three "chiefs" took twenty-four boys and three girls to an OIA school in Albuquerque. Because of widespread anxiety over the children, three headmen made several visits to the school with Patten and his successor William B. Clark in 1884. Agent Christian Stollsteimer noted in 1887, "The Indians are inordinately fond of their children, and cling to them not only through natural affection but also as the hope of their, now, almost extinct race."[20] He made no distinction between genders regarding this concern, yet there is no indication that Ute women were allowed to visit their children at school. OIA agents addressed this separation anxiety through male channels alone.

Ute women were, nevertheless, the primary force behind resistance to off-reservation schools. They told Stollsteimer that they feared the high rates of disease in governmental schools, and their concerns were well founded for, of the twenty-five Ute students sent to boarding school in Albuquerque in 1883, twelve died.[21] Ute women's objections to boarding schools prompted the OIA to open a day school at the agency in 1886, yet many women were still reticent to send their children. Stollsteimer complained, "The conducting of a school here meets with the most strenuous opposition from the squaws." The day school had only ten pupils during its brief existence, and Stollsteimer commented that both parents of these pupils came "almost daily to the agency to see them, and in many ways [showed] their anxiety." During these visits, many Utes expressed concern over the safety of the school building. The OIA agreed that the school was unsafe and closed it in 1890. The Utes were without a school until 1892, when the abandoned facilities at Fort Lewis were transformed into a boarding school.[22]

Enrollments of Ute children at the Fort Lewis boarding school were low, however, because of the continuing problem of illness. When the Utes grudgingly sent sixteen children to the school in 1894, three of them died and three returned home blind. The Utes' apprehension over their children's health, led by the women, eventually forced the OIA once again to modify its plans. In 1902 it opened the Southern Ute boarding school at the agency near Ignacio.[23]

While resistance to Fort Lewis continued, the on-reservation boarding school was, for reasons that are not quite clear, surprisingly successful. Why did Ute parents fill Southern Ute boarding school to capacity?[24] What accounted for the change in the Indians' behavior? Ute agent Joseph Smith described the parents' reactions to the opening of the school:

> A great many of the parents visited the school on the day of the opening and great care was exercised in showing them through the different apartments of the school and the purpose for which each part of

the building was used was fully explained to them. The parents stayed with their children most of the day and assisted them in bathing and dressing them, departing late in the afternoon well pleased with the school.[25]

Perhaps the school's proximity encouraged favorable feelings among parents. Perhaps the new school building alleviated their fears of disease and injury. Perhaps the agents' careful explanations of how the school functioned reassured them that their children would be well cared for. Or perhaps the parents in 1902 were simply more acculturated than the earlier group. In any case, there is no further mention of women's opposition — at least with respect to the school at Southern Ute.

The reasons for the differential success of the two schools may have had more to do with the new policies concerning school attendance than with any shift in Ute women's attitudes towards education. In 1904 the superintendent of the Fort Lewis school, William Peterson, made an agreement with Ute agent Joseph Smith to begin withholding rations from families who refused to send their children to school. In 1906 Education Circular No. 130 made this practice official. With the entire family held hostage, men and women were equally affected by the ruling.[26] The patterns of resistance that occurred after 1904, then, were probably shaped more by economic considerations than by one particular gender's (women's) concerns for the safety of their children.

At Southern Ute, where annual reports from 1904 to the 1930s noted that the school was filled to capacity, the economic penalties may have been working. At Fort Lewis, however, withholding rations and annuities failed to induce Ute parents to enroll their children. This was partially because the group closest to Fort Lewis was the unallotted Weminuches, who were far more conservative than the bands near the Southern Ute school. Yet the economic situation of the Weminuches also thwarted the effectiveness of the new sanctions. Superintendent Peterson observed that the Weminuche Utes owed all of their money to the agency trader and did not care if their funds were not forthcoming. Regardless of Peterson's economic sanctions, both men and women kept their children out of the Fort Lewis school.[27]

It is also possible that the Weminuches used (or claimed to use) Floretta Shields' mission day school near Cortez as an alternative to OIA schools. In 1906 (one year before she left the school) Peterson complained to the CIA that Shields "resists the efforts of the agency to promote schooling" by advising the Utes to put their children in her school. According to Peterson, the two largest Weminuche families claimed that their children attended Shields' school. Peterson said he never saw any children at Shields' home when he visited, but a Presbyterian colleague of Shields confirmed that she did indeed have a school with pupils.[28] Thus, Shields' institution may have served as a means of resisting government schools.

Once male OIA commissioners had established the policy of mandatory education, and Ute men had agreed to supply children, Indian women were allowed some choice in which school their children would attend. In 1902 an OIA circular granted parents the right to chose a school. It made no distinction concerning gender but rather allowed for general parental consent. Several Ute agents noted that both parents contributed their views as to the preferred location of their children's education.[29]

Head of the Household Policies

Along with excluding women from councils, delegations, and rewards for cooperating with schooling, OIA officials further sequestered women in the private sphere with "head of the house" policies. Although there were exceptions, the OIA considered men the "heads of houses" and dealt with them in all procedures concerning annuities and allotments. The 1884 regulations of the Indian Office instructed that the annuity rolls should list families "commencing with the head of the same, and followed by the names and a brief description of all the persons for whom he or she is entitled to draw the per capita." The first reference to heads of families acknowledges that this person may be female, but the second assumes that individual to be male: "heads of families receipting for the amount due them, their wives, and the minor children of their families."[30]

The 1904 OIA regulations noted, "The father and head of the family will be allowed to receive and receipt for the shares of himself, his wife, and his minor children." This edition of the regulations, however, recognized single women as heads of families able to receipt for annuities, and wives were given special privileges to sign for their shares and the shares of their children if their husbands proved to be, sick, old, or incompetent—the latter being defined as "improvident, a drunkard, a gambler, a spendthrift, or for any other reason an unfit person."[31] While OIA officials preferred to deal with men in distributing annuities and rations, they sometimes found themselves confronted by women.

In 1878 Ute agent Francis Weaver described how women participated in a campaign to intimidate him into providing more rations:

A majority of the women and children with the older men and a few chiefs arrived first. The Ute warriors and the Navajos waited below the agency until all came up, when they formed in line and approached the agency discharging their firearms. When dismounted, a clamor for rations began, especially among the women.

Weaver refused to grant the Indians' wishes, telling them he would only issue them one week's worth of rations at a time, and they left empty-handed. Three days later, the chiefs returned with a different group of women, and this time they were more cooperative:

The chiefs came back to the Agency today bringing with them six men, fourteen women, most of whom are widows of the tribe, and who were left in charge of the camp at the time of their coming for annuities, also six children.

The second delegation receipted for their shares and left quietly.[32]

The dynamics of this shifting situation are not clearly described in these documents, but it is significant that Agent Weaver commented on the inclusion of the widows (presumably older women) in the second group. Perhaps these women derided the chiefs for returning without their goods and told them they would go back to the agency with them to get the necessary items. Since Ute culture revered age over gender, these women would have felt no reluctance to behave in this manner.[33] Perhaps the women made an independent decision to return for the rations and the men were accompanying them, or perhaps the presence of older women simply had a calming effect on the chiefs. In any case, women appeared to have played an active and important role in both encounters.

Weaver's respite from Ute demands lasted only until the next ration day when, again, the Indians insisted on more food than was allocated. This time the chiefs ordered "a sack of flour for every woman," and, again, Weaver would not grant their wishes.[34] Whether the Ute women had themselves requested the extra flour is unclear. Nevertheless, the women were further involved in conflict with the agent over resources in a very public arena.

Women continued to be active in disputes over rations but the next incident seemed to indicate that men controlled the confrontations. Two weeks after the first clash, the Utes renewed their clamor for more rations. This time when Weaver still refused he noted that the Ute men "imme-diately commanded the women to leave." Weaver feared the dismissal of the women indicated violent intentions, but the men merely "lingered" at the agency and then left. Later that day, the men returned and accepted the amounts Weaver was willing to distribute.[35] Interpreting this action with respect to Ute gender behavior is problematic. From the Anglo point of view, the men ordered the women away to protect them from impending violence and the women left because they were subservient to the men's authority. But there was no violence. The men left, and then returned and accepted Weaver's amount of rations. As events did not proceed according to Weaver's fears, the Utes either backed down or they had a different agenda.

Since Ute women traditionally followed men into battle to scalp and loot, it is doubtful that the men sent them away to spare them from violence. The men may not have "commanded" the women to leave at all. The discussion preceding the women's departure may have produced two different strategies regarding the agent's recalcitrance that were, perhaps, roughly divided along gender lines. (Agent Weaver did not speak Ute and the commotion may have caused some confusion in translation.) The women's faction might have gone away of its own accord in the same way that one dissenting group often withdrew from the other in pre-reservation culture.[36]

Thus, conclusions about gender roles in public confrontations must be very carefully drawn. From the Anglo perspective, the women left as commanded and their public behavior appeared passive. From the Ute perspective, however, the women may have left as an active adaptive strategy to protest whatever the men had proposed. The fact that the men did nothing after the women departed lends some weight to this speculation. Unless the agent intimidated the Utes with a sudden impressive show of force (which he neglected to mention in his letter to the commissioner) there would have been nothing to prevent the Indians from attacking the agent once the women left — had that been their original intent.

There were no further attempts to get more rations, but the Utes expressed their displeasure with the system by passively resisting OIA protocol for distributing annuities. Weaver complained that the Utes sat silently before him at ration time and refused to give their names. Women participated in this protest. Weaver wrote several letters to OIA commissioner Ezra A. Hayt expressing his frustration and his reluctance to issue goods without the proper procedure. Eventually he relented, giving rations to nameless Indians, both male and female.[37] Thus, many women refused to allow men to be "heads" of their houses. Rather they sought their own agency in rations and annuities and they participated in public protests over OIA policies.

Women and Nativistic Responses

Women also played a public role in religious responses to the stresses of reservation life. To cope with the pressures of forced assimilation, the Utes adopted several Pan-Indian religious movements, whose ceremonies gave them some sense of control over their lives and a way to assert their identity as Native Americans. Women played an important role in these ceremonies.

The Southern Utes embraced a form of the Ghost Dance, first during the early 1870s and again in the early twentieth century. Utes who danced in this ceremony fell into trances, journeyed to the land of the dead, and returned with encouragement from their ancestors to live morally and follow Ute ways. The Utes believed that the dance brought them good health. Women and men danced the Ghost Dance.[38]

Ute leader Buckskin Charley brought the Peyote religion, otherwise known as the Native American Church, to the reservation around 1900. For the Utes, Peyotism was a curing ceremony rather than a ritual of spiritual regeneration — its more popular form. The Native American Church provided healing, solidarity, and hope for many Utes. Women were important members of the Peyote church. They made Peyote paraphernalia, served in the ritual — blessing the water that is passed around the circle of celebrants — and were accorded equal status as participants.[39]

Around 1900 the Ute Mountain Utes adopted the Sun Dance from the Northern Utes at the Uintah-Ouray reservation in Whiterocks, Utah. A Southern Ute shaman brought the dance to the other side of the reservation around 1904. Through performance of the dance, individuals gained the power to lead moral and productive lives. As in the other dances, women helped with the ceremonial preparations, danced, prayed, and were considered crucial to the success of the ritual. According to one oral history, several women also held their own Sun Dances some time during the early reservation years. The informant did not elaborate on the reasons for these separate ceremonies.[40]

Ironically, religion was one public arena in which the OIA desired women's participation. Euro-American women were active in religion and often wielded considerable influence in churches, moral reform societies, and missionary programs. The OIA hoped that Native American women would also organize "societies for promoting literary, religious, moral, and social improvement" and take a public role in promoting religion and morality on the reservation. The plan, of course, was not for Indian women to assert leadership in the "pagan" religions the OIA sought to abolish.

Rather, Indian women were supposed to help bring Christianity to their people.[41] Instead, women participated in rituals of religious regeneration that strengthened the Utes' will to oppose forced assimilation. Women also helped to resist sedentism.

Women and the Initial Resistance to Settlement

In 1880, fifteen years before the official allotment policy, Ute leaders agreed that the tribe would take up farming on individual plots and settle into permanent houses. The majority of Utes, however, refused to live in houses. By 1890 the OIA had constructed twenty-four "dwellings" for Indians, but only five were occupied. Agent H. B. Freeman noted in 1893 that the Utes were using twenty-two out of twenty-five houses. He despaired, "The Indians, with few exceptions, set their tepees in front for living purposes and use the houses for catch all of odds and ends." Forty houses stood at Southern Ute at the time when Congress passed the Hunter Act, in 1895, and Agent David A. Day, convinced the Utes would now settle into houses, gladly helped the Indians sort out their allotment tracts around those dwellings.[42]

The promise of "progress," however, had faded within five years. Writing in 1901, Agent Joseph O. Smith lamented, "a whole family of relations will reside on one small place instead of endeavoring to improve their individual allotments." By 1905, only forty Indians (out of a total of 375 allottees) lived on their land. Gradually, however, more Utes moved into houses, at least for the winter. In 1912, 132 families (out of 152 families among the allotted Utes) inhabited forty-three houses. The number of Utes living in houses fluctuated over the fifteen years, reaching a peak in 1920 when all 118 families on the reservation resided in houses. Construction of houses rose from forty-three in 1914 to eighty-three by 1929. Still, as late as 1929 many Ute families spent at least part of their summers in tepees.[43]

The Utes probably refused to settle in houses for a variety of reasons. They might have been responding to the epidemic diseases that struck the reservation during the late nineteenth century. In 1890, smallpox raged through the tribe. In 1891, a severe flu epidemic caused such panic that the agent, accused by the Utes of witchcraft, feared for his life. An outbreak of catarrh decimated Ute ranks in 1892. In the face of high death rates due to these diseases, the Ute custom of abandoning houses where deaths occurred may account for their shunning of these abodes. Moreover, the continuation of traditional Ute hunting and gathering subsistence patterns discouraged sedentism.[44]

Ute women were vital to the tribe's resistance to sedentism. Their labor in gathering plants and berries and in moving camps was essential to a continued semi-nomadic existence. Women were the primary individuals who maintained ties with family and friends in other locations. Perusal of agents' letters on inheritance hearings, annuity roll matters, and individual Indian bank accounts indicates a tremendous amount of movement between the Southern Ute agency and both the Navajo Springs agency and the Uintah-Ouray agency in Whiterocks, Utah. In addition, fifty-seven letters written by agents for Southern Utes to Northern Utes between 1883 and 1893 testify to the cross-reservation ties maintained by Ute bands. The letters talk of marriages, births, deaths, and the health of family members, inquire after friends and loved ones, plan Bear Dances, and discuss recent and future visits. Women requested the majority of these dispatches, highlighting their role in preserving family ties.[45]

For the Indians allotted at Southern Ute, these connections created a regional community beyond their allotted lands. The Southern Ute bands made lengthy visits to other jurisdictions and intermarried with the Weminuche and Northern Utes to the point where "they do not know themselves which tribe they belong to." The Utes' continual shifting of residences, either through extended visits or marriage, frustrated OIA assimilation plans. Agents Burton B. Custer, in 1905, William D. Leonard, in 1906, and Walter G. West, in 1916 and 1917, despaired that the Southern Utes' continual absences from the reservation and their contact with the unallotted Weminuches retarded their "progress."[46] The Utes' defiance of OIA attempts to settle them onto farms thwarted every aspect of OIA assimilationist plans. This option existed, in large part, because of kinship ties maintained by women.

Conclusions

On the Southern Ute reservation, the OIA granted the role of public leadership, however limited by the reservation context, to male Indians. All official correspondence regarding public decision making with the Utes focused on interactions with men. Agents called on men to implement every major tenet of the Dawes Act — settlement on the reservation, allotments, and the education of children. OIA officials did not consult Ute women at any time in the creation or administration of the reservation.

They did not debate women's place in the new society; they simply assumed it to be private and secondary to that of men. Women were excluded from the fundamental political structures of the reservation.

For Ute women this represented a dramatic departure from their previous social position. Accustomed to participating in public decisions, or at least having the right to withdraw if they could not get their views accepted, they refused to sit back silently and allow Anglo and Ute men to dictate their activities. They publicly criticized and resisted OIA policies. They offered opinions, both positive and negative, in every area of public life: removal, allotments, annuities, and education. In short, they refused to be relegated to a private domestic role. Ute women participated in homemaking activities with Anglo women, but they did not embrace the "separate sphere" ideals of Anglo gender roles.

THREE

Women and Economics

Under the Dawes Act, the OIA designed the reservation economy so that men would become self-sufficient farmers or laborers and women would be homemakers, financially dependent on wage-earning men. OIA policy limited women's educational training to domestic skills, aimed at producing homemakers, and underscored women's dependency by giving family allotments to husbands, not wives, in the first generation of allottees. The plan to create a gendered economy, both patriarchal and middle class in its conception, collided both with the poor reservation economy and Ute ideas of women as producers who made, owned, and disposed of their own property as they pleased.

Dependency and the Reservation Economy

OIA policy makers approached the restructuring of Native American economies with racist and sexist assumptions about Indians' potential productivity. Many officials felt the Indians' "innate laziness" was the primary hindrance to Office plans. In their annual reports, several agents at Southern Ute noted that one reason Ute men were so "lazy" was that the women did all the work. Agent Francis Weaver noted in 1877 that Ute men "Will do nothing and say their fathers lived without work and why not they. The women . . . are no better off than slaves, subject to all the work and drudgery imaginable." In 1879 Agent Henry M. Page commented that the Utes considered labor "degrading and only to be performed by whites and 'squaws.'" In 1881, observing several Ute families preparing to move their

37

camps, he reiterated these sentiments. "The squaws," he wrote, "[did] all the labor required" to move their camps. Agent Charles Bartholomew agreed with these assessments, concluding, in 1891, that Ute men's "disposition is generally indolent" for Ute women did the work.[1] The Office concluded that agents should persuade Indian men to earn a living and not rely on their wives.

In reality, even men who wanted to support their wives could not because the government failed to properly sustain the reservation economy. The reservation had no irrigation ditches until 1887, twenty-seven years after its establishment. A lack of firm water rights was also a problem. Although the Office awarded the Utes money in 1905 for purchase of "perpetual water rights," neighboring non-Ute farmers continually challenged their claims to water, and irrigation was never adequate. The removal controversy during 1890 and 1891 also blocked farming efforts. David A. Day, agent at the time of allotments (1895), blamed the Utes' lack of "advancement" on congressional politics, which held up issuance of the proper seeds and implements. He wrote, in 1894, "Farming here, with possibly four exceptions, is a farce for which Congress alone is responsible." By 1913, eighteen years after allotment, Agent Charles Werner could only point to twenty-four families who were "practically self-supporting."[2]

Since irrigation water was lacking but there seemed to be abundant grazing acreage, sheep appeared to be the ideal project for the Utes. Yet the livestock industry at Southern Ute was never successful beyond the subsistence level. In 1913 Charles Davis, supervisor of farming, and Seldon K. Emerson, agency farmer, both noted that the Indians' herds were too small to be profitable and suggested government seed money to remedy this. The OIA, however, did not approve the seed money to bolster the sheep industry until 1928.[3]

Economic conditions surrounding the reservation also affected Ute self-sufficiency. Charles Werner, in 1910, and Agent Edward McKean, in 1918, complained that the cost of living was expensive and railroad rates high in southern Colorado. In 1922 OIA inspector John Atwater concluded that because of "the depression in the price of farm products and the high freight rates, [the Indians'] crops are not remunerative at this time."[4]

With their chances of becoming successful farmers or stockmen often hindered by economic forces beyond their control, most Ute men who worked performed wage labor. During the summers of 1907–9, some Ute "men and large boys" worked in the beet fields at Rocky Ford, Colorado, under the auspices of the OIA outing-work program, but low wages and poor working conditions eventually ended their participation. Because local ranchers and businessmen declined to hire Utes except for irrigation work in the spring, agency wage work was really the only source of income for Ute men. Agency jobs for men included laborer, interpreter, policeman, engineer, or clerk. These latter positions, however, were civil service jobs and no Ute men qualified for them.[5] For Native American husbands to support nonworking wives required a stable and reasonably prosperous income for Indian men; the reservation economy was never sufficient for this task.

Divorce, Property, and Female Dependency

The lack of an adequate base upon which to build an economy of dependent women was not the only obstacle the policy makers faced. Ute conceptions of women's productive value also hindered the creation of a gendered economy. A case study of divorce and property rights contrasts Ute and OIA perceptions of women's economic roles.

The allotment policies of the Dawes Act reflected the OIA's vision of economic gender roles. The act excluded married women from receiving allotments (unless they were married to men outside their tribes or were under eighteen years of age) but allowed single, divorced, and widowed women to obtain land. Although wives had no land of their own, the Office viewed them as co-owners with their husbands. The agents recorded the wife's name next to her husband's to indicate that, while she was not "counted or numbered on the schedule as an allottee," the land allotted to her husband was also hers. This provision was supposed to hold for couples married by tribal custom; a legal marriage license was not required if the two were man and wife before allotment.[6]

Laws regulating Indian marriages, however, were convoluted. Native Americans residing on reservations during the Dawes era were subject to two legal jurisdictions—federal and state. Because there was no federal law circumscribing marriage and divorce, the OIA allowed noncitizen Indians to follow tribal practices. Nevertheless, women without legal documents were left without property if their marriages ended because the granting of allotments affected the legal status of their marital bonds. Cato Sells, the CIA in 1917, ruled that the allotment process itself negated the legality of tribal marriages because Indians became citizens by accepting allotments. He wrote: "While Indians maintain tribal relations they may marry and divorce themselves but not after they become citizens."[7] Commissioner Sells was clear on the question of wives' marital property rights: without a legal marriage, divorced women had no claims on their former families' property. Therefore, Indian women could only take advantage of state laws concerning married women's property if they had legal marriages.

In the case of Southern Ute women with state-sanctioned marriages, state law clearly protected their rights to certain kinds of property. The Colorado civil code safeguarded the property a woman brought into a marriage or earned or inherited afterwards. Allotments fell under these provisions, provided they were assigned to the women. Thus, on the reservation, single women, widows, wives under the age of eighteen, and wives of non-Utes owned their allotments. Legally wed, co-allotted wives did not have ownership rights over the allotments assigned to their husbands, but they could probably claim some lands under divorce and alimony statutes. Ute women with tribally sanctioned marriages, however, had no rights to alimony.

Unless they were immediately married by the state, wives in this first generation of allottees had no claims to their families' property. Commissioner Sells admitted that the OIA's position sometimes hurt Indian women but imagined that the ex-husbands would share their property at the request of the reservation superintendents.[8] In the reservation family, then, most wives were completely subject to their husbands' decisions on property ownership.

Southern Ute women whose marriages remained intact were untouched by limitations on their property rights, but divorced women suffered. The Bureau of Land Management allotment book listed a total of sixty-one wives, all designated as co-allottees. Of these women, forty-six remained married until one of the partners died. Twenty-eight were widowed, nine were divorced, and six are untraceable in the records. All of the twenty-eight widows inherited the husband's allotment, but in the instances of divorce, the co-allotted wives found they had no legal claims to the land they supposedly shared with their husbands.[9]

There were ten divorce actions among the original allottees at Southern Ute from 1905 to 1917, eight of which involved an appeal by the woman to the agent for a land settlement. The reasoning behind the women's actions is not exactly clear. In pre-reservation Ute culture, a woman wishing a divorce either left her husband or asked him to leave. A lack of real property (in the Euro-American sense) and the semi-nomadic economy meant that women probably did not ask their husbands for anything when they ended their marriages. While pre-reservation women never owned land, they did have property rights over anything they made, including tepees. Perhaps they extended this concept of ownership to their new homes. The question remains, however, if expecting part of the allotment when they left their husbands was the equivalent of asking for alimony? Did it indicate that they were now expecting their ex-husbands to support them? Is this evidence that they had internalized the ideology of dependency?[10]

An examination of the eight divorce cases yields some insight into the women's property claims. In 1906 Agent William D. Leonard wrote to the CIA on behalf of four women co-allottees. The women had been married by tribal law and were now divorced, also by tribal law, and their husbands had remarried. Leonard asked that Sarah Buck, Peggy Washington, Ada Russell, and Daisy Baker be given a portion of their husbands' allotments, for their listing on the allotment rolls legitimated their claims. The outcome for these four women was either bad or uncertain. Sarah Buck and Daisy Baker never got any land; the documents do not mention what happened to Ada Russell and Peggy Washington.[11]

In four other cases, ex-wives received land. Benjamin North deeded 160 acres of land to his former wife Elmira. In 1916 John Tyler presented his ex-spouse Anne with some land and, in 1917, Alfonso Kuebler paid his "discarded" wife $500, even though she was legally entitled to nothing. In 1917 Topsy Plato's divorce decree noted that her former mate had ceded forty acres to his minor children "as a settlement of any claim which [Topsy] might have on his property." Topsy was not a co-allottee, having married John Tyler after his divorce from Anne. Although Topsy's settlement gave the land to her children by John Tyler, the property was in effect hers, for she lived on it until her death.[12]

The reasons for these women's successes are not clear from the documents, nor do the agents record the women's view of their property rights. The women's good fortune may have been due to Agent Walter West's persuasive personality or to their husbands' generosity. There is no evidence that the agent brought sanctions against any of these husbands. In all of these cases, the only issue mentioned in the granting of land is children. Since Topsy was not Tyler's wife at the time of allotment, her children would not have been assigned land with their father. Apparently, however, all the parties involved agreed that they should receive a portion of their father's holdings. Topsy gained her property only indirectly — by virtue of being the children's mother rather than by having been John's wife.

The records do not indicate whether Topsy appealed for land on this basis, but Ute interpretations of parental obligations might have encouraged her to do so. While there are no ethnographic accounts of "child support" payments in pre-reservation Ute culture, there was considerable emphasis on family responsibilities to offspring. The rites of passage surrounding birth underscored the father's role in caring for his children. After the birth of a child, the newborn's grandparents (or older relatives acting as grandparents) ate a ritual meal with the father, admonishing him to provide for the child, and blessing him to increase his hunting ability. After the meal, the father went on a "mock hunt" lasting several days. During this ritual he ran frantically through the surrounding countryside in the exaggerated motions of a skillful hunter. This ceremony ensured that he would have the speed and endurance to be a successful provider.[13]

Additionally, in the Ute concept of family, children belonged to all consanguineal lines — each of which contributed to the tasks of feeding, clothing, and enculturating the child. Utes believed that a child might have more than one father, for they thought that conception occurred when, over time, semen *(wana'tepi)* filled up an amniotic sac *(no'gup)*. Thus, residence in the immediate family did not necessarily restrict the obligations to a child. This reasoning may have motivated women to press for property after they were no longer living with their husbands.[14]

Another Ute wife attempted to get a property settlement based on her role as a mother, but where Topsy Plato succeeded, Daisy Spencer Baker failed. Her case is especially illuminating because she left letters concerning her divorce. Daisy's struggle against her ex-husband James Baker began in 1905 when Agent Burton B. Custer posted a notice: "Daisy Spencer — former wife of James Baker — has no control whatever of the land allotted to them jointly [and] those who trespass do so at their own risk and will be handled according to law."[15] There is no record of her response to this message but since the agents' annual reports did not record any trouble with trespassing over the next decade, she probably respected the warning.

She did not, however, accept the idea that she had no claim to the family property. In 1916 Agent Walter West replied to a letter she had sent him asking about her two dead children's allotments. He explained that the secretary of the interior had declared James Baker sole heir to the allotments. In June of 1917, Daisy wrote to the commissioner herself demanding half of Baker's land because "we were allotted together and now we are not living together. he *[sic]* has said that he did not take me as his wife as i *[sic]* think he should give me -½ of the 320 acres he has." She told the commissioner that she had asked the Southern Ute agent to write but that she doubted he had. She concluded, "Do with me what you think the best."[16]

Agent Edward E. McKean took up Daisy's cause in a letter to the OIA in 1917. While Daisy had no legal claims on James Baker's land, he felt that she "would be greatly assisted in supporting herself" if the Office would deed her a portion. The commissioner responded by explaining that, since Indian marriages and divorces were not valid after "they [became] citizens by allotment or otherwise," James Baker owed his wife nothing; he suggested that McKean try to persuade him to deed "the Indian" some land. James refused, however, in the process making some derogatory remarks regarding his ex-wife.[17]

Daisy responded to these remarks in a letter to McKean in January of 1918. She accused the commissioner and McKean of siding with her former husband "just so we will be quarrelling *[sic]* about it." Apparently James reiterated that Daisy had never been his wife and that he was not the father of her children. She expressed wounded outrage at these charges:

> Jim Baker says with his own tongue I was not his wife, he says he just lived with me like any lose *[sic]* animal. What more worse name can he give me than to call me an animal[?] If I was an lose *[sic]* animal what does he want my land for he makes fun of me. . . . I had my children and this man who says he was not my husband gets all the money out of them and I don't get any one penny. it *[sic]* is because you say he is heir. He want *[sic]* to be the heir but he don't want to take children as his children.

Three times Daisy demanded her land and she ended her letter by claiming, "I am going to get my land some way if you can't do."[18]

Some time after Daisy's angry letter, Baker capitulated and offered her 160 acres if she would sign a statement relinquishing any future demands on the rest of his land. Daisy, obviously still smarting from his earlier accusations of promiscuity, refused to sign the waiver. "I don't want to give my childs *[sic]* land to Jim Baker. he *[sic]* says they are not his children. Before I sign anything like this I will go to court with him." She demanded more land because she had several children. The commissioner instructed McKean to "have a talk with the Indian and with James Baker and see if some satisfactory settlement cannot be made."[19] No further letters are available, but evidently Daisy never got her land.

When James Baker died at the age of seventy-seven (on August 13, 1927), his personal papers listed four wives including Daisy's sister Eliza (who died in 1907), who may have been married to James at the same time as her sister. The papers note that Daisy died in 1920 and had no land.[20] For all her efforts on behalf of herself and her children, Daisy Spencer Baker died with nothing — an example of the economic vulnerability of married women, particularly tribally married women, under the Euro-American definitions of gender roles.

The stories of Topsy Plato and Daisy Baker provide a glimpse of women's perceptions of their rights within the family — Daisy's by direct statement and Topsy's by implication. Both women's claims rested primarily on their roles as mother rather than on those as wife. Perhaps the women felt that the former claim would carry more weight with the agent than the latter, or perhaps the argument reflected the women's own view of what their husbands owed them. Were they asking for "support" in the Euro-American sense? Was this a middle ground where OIA agents and Ute women agreed that women and children should be supported by men? While reservation personnel seemed to hold the latter position, an examination of Ute ideology of gender and familial obligations suggests that Ute women viewed the situation differently. In traditional Ute culture a woman's identity was closely tied to her reproductive functions. Women's power to give life was celebrated in birthing rituals and emphasized in menstrual practices. The idea that a woman's value was tied to motherhood also appears in myth. In some myths women take part in the initial creation of life. Specific tales depicting women as mothers are also very complimentary. While the mythic portrayal of Ute women as wives or sexual partners is not always flattering, Ute mothers are brave, selfless, and resourceful — at least with regard to their own children.[21]

In short, the role of mother gave women dignity and identity. Reproductive success was important to the Utes, and they had a type of fertility dance called the Bear Dance. According to mythology, a bear once told a Ute hunter that he would improve his sexual and hunting abilities if he performed a dance to propitiate bears. The dance, held in the spring, when bears ended their hibernation and the earth was once again fertile, functioned as a courtship ritual. In pre-contact times, it could also mark the end of a girl's puberty ritual.[22] The Utes, therefore, sought supernatural aid and blessing in areas crucial to their survival — hunting and producing children. Ute culture valued and celebrated both roles equally.

A woman's children were her highly valued accomplishments. To be a mother was, for Ute women, to be a fully participating member of Ute society. Daisy Baker's words "I had my children" probably meant "I have fulfilled my adult role in this society — I count." Her demand for land was probably based on the idea that she, as a productive adult, should be allowed equal access to the new subsistence base. While she may have felt her husband had an obligation to her children, she probably did not assume he had an obligation to provide for her once their marriage was over. Her request was most likely an attempt to secure resources in order to care for herself and her children.

Southern Ute agents agreed that divorced women should have a share of the reservation resources, but they viewed this right from a different perspective. The OIA *Rulebook*, first published in 1883, established sanctions for husbands who refused to support their families. An offender in this regard lost his rations until he proved to the agent that he would provide for his family. The OIA, then, demanded men support their wives if the family remained intact, but placed the question of ex-wives' access to family assets under the jurisdiction of local courts. The 1881 and 1891 statute laws of Colorado allowed women to sue for divorce on the grounds of impotency, adultery, cruelty, drunkenness, desertion, or failure to provide, and they made provision for a woman to receive alimony and child support (if she got custody of the children) not in excess of $2,000 or half her husband's income.[23] Agent McKean considered Daisy's petition for land in the context of Colorado laws codifying a husband's obligation to provide alimony for dependent wives and children. He viewed the allotments as properly belonging to James, and Daisy's claim on them as that of a dependent.[24]

While Anglo agents and Ute women envisioned women's property rights from very different perspectives, they seemed to agree that the women had legitimate claims. Further, although the concept of "mother" meant divergent things to each side, both the agents and the women put forward the women's requests in the context of their maternal role. The idea of motherhood functioned as a middle ground in land negotiations in which women challenged gendered differential access to resources.[25]

Education, Gender Roles, and Economic Opportunity

Strict Euro-American gender roles also underlay the vocational training offered in OIA schools. Boys learned farming and mechanical trades in the expectancy of earning a living, while girls acquired homemaking skills in the expectancy of being supported by a husband. Girls' education occurred in the classroom, in the demonstration "playhouse" constructed at the Southern Ute boarding school in 1910, and also in that school's dormitory. OIA inspectors' reports of the Southern Ute boarding school, the Allen day school, and the Fort Lewis boarding school (which had few Utes) indicated general observance of these guidelines.[26]

Policies governing the operation of OIA schools also underscored the

ideology of female economic dependency. The children performed all tasks
necessary to run the school according to a strict gender division of labor —
girls did the housekeeping and boys cared for the school farms, stock, and
mechanical equipment. For girls at Southern Ute, this meant long hours of
work, for which they were never paid. Indian girls in the Southern Ute
boarding school sewing shop made aprons, pillow cases, curtains, clothing,
sheets, towels, napkins, and table cloths, the total goods ranging in worth
from $195 to $1300 per year. These items were not sold but were used by
the school. In contrast, the product of the schoolboys' labor — farm produce — was sold for cash. The unspoken message of this policy was that
boys labored for wages while girls' work went to household subsistence.[27]

Agents Walter West and Edward McKean also organized after-school
clubs, in 1916 and 1918 respectively, to drive home women's domestic
roles. West's girls' club emphasized sewing, and McKean added cooking,
rug, and flower clubs. The eleven members of the garden club focused on
"beautifying the home by planting and caring for an individual flower garden by each member." Likewise, members of the rug club dedicated themselves to decorating with "beautiful and useful rugs from old clothing."[28]

At least two reservation superintendents attempted to train the girls at
Southern Ute school to be "ladies" as well as good homemakers. In 1906
William Leonard requested money to buy a piano for the girls. Leonard
appeared to be following suggestions of Merial Dorchester, Indian School
Service special agent, who wrote, in 1891, "There is no instrumentality
more civilizing than music." Walter West, in 1916, requested funds to buy
corsets to improve "the general health and appearance of the girls."[29] Corsets and piano lessons represented the Euro-American ideal of decorative
passivity for women and highlighted the ideal of female dependency.

Although the OIA sought to train the women to become wives of "progressive young Indians," a few schoolgirls used their training for wage
work. From about 1905 to 1913, many women in Colorado and Utah wrote
to the Fort Lewis school requesting Indian women to work as domestic
servants. The school superintendents, William Peterson and his successor
John S. Spear (who arrived in 1906), seemed careful about policing the
system for abuses. They demanded letters of reference from the families
requesting an Indian domestic and explained to them their duty to be a
"good influence" for the young ladies in their homes. They also assured
Indian parents that their daughters had good homes and that any girl with
the slightest complaint would be brought back to the reservation.[30]

In reality, John Spear was not as conscientious regarding the girls' welfare as he claimed. In July of 1906 Miss Lucy Head, a Southern Ute girl,

wrote to him asking to be removed from the home where she was working. He replied with a very condescending letter alternately dismissing her feelings and telling her, "I want you to write me whenever you have anything to tell me." He promised to come and investigate the situation. The same day he wrote to her employers, a Mr. and Mrs. Carr, explaining that Lucy had asked to come home, but assuring them that he did not take her sentiments seriously, "for I know what small matters will upset Indian girls." He closed by requesting that they not tell Lucy he had written to them.[31]

Lucy's parents came to Fort Lewis to get their daughter and to confront Spear about some unkind remarks he had earlier made about their home. Spear was away from the reservation at the time of their visit, but he sent them a letter regretting that he had missed them and apologizing for his remarks. "It may be that I was misinformed in regard to your character and the kind of home you have," he wrote to Lucy's father, "and if so I am sorry, I do not wish to do injustice to anyone, nor do I wish any child to neglect, forget, or in any way slight their parents." He urged them to allow their daughter to remain in school and outing work, but promised to return her if they so desired.[32]

Spear tried to transfer Lucy to another Mancos farmer, but the arrangement fell through when he could not find the Carrs another Indian servant. Lucy then ran away from the Carrs, much to Spear's annoyance, and he remarked that she should go ahead and leave her job so that she could "learn when she was well-off." His closing statement in this affair indicated the reality of outing work in southern Colorado: "Should I move the girls every time they become dissatisfied and make a complaint to me, it would not be long until no one would want them."[33] Although the superintendents claimed they were placing the girls in beneficial situations, this remark suggests that many of the girls did not agree.

There were at least two other recorded incidents of friction between Indian domestics and their mistresses. In letters to prospective employers of Indian women, Peterson noted in 1905 and 1906 that several unnamed Indian women were unhappy in their positions, and apparently some of them left their employers without permission. Perhaps because of these incidents, outing work appears to have gradually decreased after 1906. By 1913 Agent Stephen Abbott told the CIA, "there are very few, if any, homes in this vicinity in which [Indian] girls would be received as workers and accorded kindly consideration." Abbott did not explain why women near the reservation stopped requesting Indian servants, but Ute women apparently became disenchanted with the system as well. In 1914 Superintendent West told a woman from Victor, Colorado, that no Ute girls were inter-

ested in working as domestics "for the reason that most of them can earn
$1.50 per day here at home while not at work on their farms." He did not
say how the women earned this money.[34]

One Ute woman, however, did extensive outing work after graduating
from the Indian school in Santa Fe, New Mexico. Nancy Shoshone was an
orphan. Her sister and legal guardian, May Shoshone Gunn, enrolled her
in the Santa Fe school in 1912. Nancy finished her studies in 1916 and took
a position with Mrs. M. L. Burrows in Santa Fe. In January of 1917, she
wrote to Agent West requesting a job at the reservation boarding school.
West replied that he had no openings, but he recommended her and her
sister Flora for maids' jobs at the Arlington Hotel in Pagosa Springs, Colorado, near the reservation. Nancy elected to stay in Santa Fe until June of
1917 when she became a domestic servant in Durango, Colorado, also near
the reservation.[35]

Holding her job in Santa Fe for a year, and later working in Durango,
Nancy had obviously internalized the work ethic that OIA administrators
hoped to impose on Indian men. Nevertheless, she struggled with homesickness, low pay, and tasks she disliked in her job. In January of 1917 she
wrote to Superintendent Snyder of the Santa Fe school:

> This is Monday afternoon as I thought I would write to you again as I
> have written to [Agent] West [a] week ago to asked *[sic]* him if I could
> go home. Just [on] account of my spells as I get so tired of myself been
> so much troubles with my rheumatism [in] all of my joints . . . but I am
> so homesick while I am sick.[36]

Nancy assured both Snyder and West that she was not lazy. "I love to work
very much," she wrote, "but here I don't earn anything and I can't make
anything out of it." The death of Nancy's grandfather in February of 1917
intensified her homesickness. She wrote:

> I heard my grandfather died and I am very lonesome, especially when I
> didn't see him. So I want to go home and see about my grandmother
> and how she is getting along. . . . Well, Mr. West, I am *[sic]* cer-
> tainly missed my grandfather. it *[sic]* makes me so homesick when
> I heard of [how] my poor grandfather died and now I wanted to
> go home.[37]

West, Snyder, and Nancy agreed she would return home in June. In May of
1917 she wrote to Snyder expressing ambivalence about her job ending.

I am thanking you very much for you got me a nice people to work for and I like them too but I only got very tired working now. . . . If I happen to come back to this place I want to work for some other people. I don't like to take care of children very much.

Despite her letter, Nancy apparently meant to return to Mrs. Burrows, for she left her trunk full of her belongings.[38]

Near the end of August, she wrote to both Mrs. Burrows and Superintendent Snyder informing them that family concerns had motivated her to remain on the reservation and asking that they forward her things.

I thought I would like to write to you to let you know that I am not going back down to Santa Fe this fall as my sister Mrs. May Gunn and her husband are not getting along very well. . . . Also I am helping my sister to make things for exhibit working for the fair this fall on Sept. the 20th next month. . . . Say Mr. Snyder I left my trunk at Mrs. Burrows [sic] house and I want you to help me to send my trunk in.

Superintendent Snyder returned her trunk and Nancy took a servant's job in Durango.[39]

After moving to Durango, Nancy tried to secure employment for her sisters Flora, Jane, and Edith. "I don't want them to stay home just to run around like J. C. and A. W.," she wrote to Edward McKean in 1918, "I want my sisters to earn something and learn what's right." McKean agreed to send the girls when the term ended at the boarding school, and Nancy wrote back that he should also send her cousin Anna Weaver, as she had found a job for her at Mercy Hospital in Durango. She promised to take good care of her family.[40] Government records do not indicate whether Nancy's relatives ever joined her in Durango.

Nancy translated her homemaking training into a labor commodity. She never put her abilities to the use the OIA intended, however, for she died of influenza in 1919 before she could ever marry. Agents who believed that the purpose of women's reservation education was not the impartation of employable skills but indoctrination in domesticity must have been pleased that so few women took jobs as domestic servants. In contrast, those middle- and upper-class women in the region who viewed the reservation as a pool of cheap labor must have been disappointed. As to the Ute women, they were forced to work in the reservation schools but they did not become an exploited class of laborers in the surrounding community — they had other options.[41]

Women's Work and Economic Activities at Southern Ute

Despite the OIA's desire to turn them into dependent wives, Ute women actively participated in economic and subsistence activities on the reservation. In addition to continuing pre-reservation gathering of wild foods and adapting old skills to reservation wage work, Ute women also utilized their limited land resources to support themselves and their families. Given the poverty of the reservation, women's subsistence work made a significant contribution to their families' survival.

In the early years of the reservation, Ute women continued seasonal food-gathering migrations. Southern Ute agents received numerous complaints of Utes "roaming about with their squaws." Many of the local Anglos feared the Ute hunting and gathering expeditions, but the forays were generally peaceful. Long after the Utes settled into houses, women often gathered and processed wild foods for their families. Several elderly women recounting oral histories in the 1980s and 1990s recalled their mothers gathering berries.[42]

Women also gardened and cared for poultry, sheep, and goats. Agent Werner reported in 1910, "many women have garden patches from one-quarter to one acre." According to statistical reports, the Utes owned varying numbers of chickens, turkeys, hogs, pigs, boars, sheep, goats, and bees. While sheep raising was always more prevalent among the unallotted Utes at Ute Mountain, the agency farmer for Southern Ute in 1931, Albert J. Floyd, remarked that seventy-six out of 100 farms at Southern Ute had sheep and "very few don't have poultry for their own use, although they do sell some eggs."[43]

OIA personnel believed that domestic animals would entwine women's affections with their homes. Edward McKean explained the ideological importance of caring for domestic animals when he introduced Belgian hares to the reservation. "It tends," he wrote, "to create a certain interest in the home, that is not furnished by other means." At Southern Ute, women's role in caring for animals developed gradually. The 1915 Home Economics supervisor Elsie E. Newton thought the Ute women "indifferent" to the use and care of domestic animals and Inspector Snyder, in 1917, commented that the Indians' chickens were finally beginning to get the attention they needed, for "on my former visits here the chickens were noticeably neglected." By 1931 some observers noted that Ute women cared for the sheep while the men farmed. OIA stockman J. B. Ulebree, however, commented that "the whole family works with the sheep," not just the women or children.[44] Animal husbandry, then, was probably not an exclusively female job among the Southern Utes.

While women tended domestic animals among the allotted Utes, men attended to them among the unallotted. In the early 1930s, Chief John Miller of the Ute Mountain Council told Agent Peacore not to speak to his men about farming, "For they are not women — they are stock raisers." In contrast to the bands on the Pine River, the unallotted Utes had much larger herds in this period, and men did most of the work with them.[45]

The explanation of the differing patterns probably lies in the two groups' new subsistence bases. Among the unallotted Utes stock raising replaced hunting as the primary subsistence task for men; farming may have been associated with gathering among these Indians, hence their scorn of it as a woman's activity.[46] Since men among the allotted Utes focused their efforts on agriculture and wage labor, they did not have time for full-time stock raising and thus they left the task to their wives. Agents may have pressured women to do this work, but it is also possible that the women wanted to do it. Whether from necessity or choice, women seemed eager to be economically productive on the reservation.

In the new reservation economy, women found they had some traditional skills with market value. In 1879 the agency hired three women as laborers to help with the construction of buildings. They were paid 25 cents per day; the male laborers were paid 50 cents per day. While the pay vouchers do not specify exactly what work the women performed, it probably involved some kind of carrying or digging, both of which were labors Ute women had performed in pre-reservation years. In 1919 the agency again hired a woman as a laborer in the "construction and repair of buildings"; she earned $200.[47]

One Ute woman, A. B., worked as an interpreter on the reservation. She was the only Southern Ute woman who was ever officially on the agency payroll. The daughter of an Apache man and a Southern Ute woman, she attended the Southern Ute boarding school from 1911 to 1913.[48] She disappeared from the records from 1913 until 1916 when she was hired as an interpreter for the field matron at Southern Ute (who went into Indian women's homes to train them in the arts of Euro-American domesticity).

A. B.'s job was a type of intermediary position in which she acted to facilitate communication between the two cultures. Her upbringing in a home where her parents came from different cultural traditions may have suited her to this job. Moreover, the intermediary role was not new for Ute women. The Utes had a woman intermediary in the style of Pocahontas: Chief Ouray's sister Susan successfully pleaded with her people for humane treatment of three Anglo women captured at the 1878 Meeker Massacre in northern Colorado. Susan was married to Johnson, the chief of the Northern Utes who had carried out the uprising against their agent Nathan Meeker. Her sympathies for the Anglo women may have been linked to her rescue from a band of Arapahos by Anglo army troops in 1864. Other intermediary roles for women before confinement to the reservation included trading their baskets and bead work with outside groups, and intermarriage with Hispanics and non-Ute Indians.[49] In these contacts, however, women acted on behalf of themselves or their tribe. A. B.'s position was different.

The OIA hired her to implement assimilationist programs. Thus, her role as cultural mediator, while similar in form to the pre-reservation pattern, was set up to function differently. It is not clear, however, how well this position worked, for there are no records describing A. B.'s work or the Ute women's reactions to her. Agent Walter West claimed the women responded well to the matron, Martha Morris, but did not credit A. B. for her help. Nevertheless, West must have felt A. B.'s work was important, for she earned $300 per year, more than the Indian male who worked as agency interpreter for $240. The commissioner remarked on this, but West did not account for the discrepancy. Whether A. B. demanded this salary or West offered it is unknown. She left for the Santa Fe Indian school in 1917 and the position of field matron's interpreter was abolished. Again, there is no explanation for either of these events.[50] Besides A. B., no other Ute women held regular agency employment. The agency did, however, occasionally encourage women in some forms of limited self-employment to supplement their husbands' incomes.

Ute women had a long tradition of craft work that was highly regarded by collectors of Indian art. They tanned deerskins for clothing and pouches, and decorated them with beads and quill embroidery. They also made baskets. Women traded or sold these items, setting their own prices and controlling the terms of the trade. The OIA, however, seemed ambivalent about this practice. On one hand, some agents encouraged craft work because it did not take the women away from the home. On the other, it was a talent used for decorating traditional clothing and household items that the Office was trying to replace with Euro-American material culture.[51] Generally, the OIA did not officially recognize the tourist trade as a viable source of reservation income. Some individual agents, however, did.

In 1910 Charles Werner noted that "many squaws do bead work. Many tourists visit the reservation and offer good prices for anything of value." Encouraged by the prospect of a thriving tourist trade, Werner hoped to bring in Apache women to revive the lost art of weaving willow baskets. Perhaps because of Werner's emphasis on women's craft work, the annual statistical reports for the reservation showed 100 women producing bead work valued at $1,000 in 1911. Agents Walter Runke (in 1913 and 1914) and Walter West (from 1915 to 1917) both dismissed women's craft work as negligible. Agent Edward McKean, who served from 1918 to 1926, advocated women's crafts. His annual reports from 1919 to 1921 list thirty women as bead workers. Twenty worked in 1922, and twenty-six in 1925. Also in 1925, twenty-five women were weaving baskets valued at $500.[52] The reports do not indicate where, if anywhere, these items were sold.

In 1931 Superintendent E. J. Peacore promoted the production and sale of beaded rabbits' feet, which he sold both on the reservation and at the United States Indian school at Mt. Pleasant, Michigan. The school in turn distributed them to local gift shops. Peacore's enthusiasm for the project was great. (Peacore's letters offer no explanation for why the Mt. Pleasant school was interested in Ute crafts.) He appeared to have supervised the work himself, ordering large quantities of beads and contacting other OIA superintendents in efforts to locate buckskin.[53]

Apart from sporadic efforts by individual agents, the federal government did not systematically and consistently encourage native crafts until the Public Works of Art project under the Indian Reorganization Act of 1934. Nevertheless, during the 1920s the CFWC tried to stimulate craft work at Southern Ute. In 1926 the CFWC appointed Nellie Wiegel chair of Indian Welfare for the state of Colorado, and she began promoting Ute crafts.[54]

Wiegel had made the study and encouragement of Ute material culture a primary concern of her long career as a Colorado clubwoman. Her interest in Native culture led her, in 1926, to attempt to procure congressional funding for an Indian crafts museum and cultural center in Durango, Colorado. Agent Edward McKean agreed to help her, and she sent craft supplies to the reservation for the Ute artists.[55] The center never materialized.

Assimilation policy was probably behind the center's failure, even as it was behind policies limiting Indian participation in fairs and Wild West Shows, another potential market for Ute women's crafts. As early as 1882, organizers of fairs, carnivals, and parades wrote to the reservation from all over Colorado and New Mexico to request Indians for their functions. The letters frequently stressed that the agent send "squaws and papooses" with "tepees and paraphernalia to camp and give exhibitions" in a recreated Indian village. The promoters always paid for transportation and food and they often paid a small fee; they always allowed the Indians to sell "trinkets, beads, etc." at the villages.[56]

Fearing that the shows caused Indians "to revive and exhibit just the things that the department is trying to eliminate from [their] lives," agents allowed attendance only if the Utes agreed to demonstrate how much "progress" they had made under OIA guidance. Consequently, the Utes took cooking, sewing, and blacksmithing demonstrations to these events. The Utes accepted these restrictions but set limits of their own; they refused to participate if they felt they were not compensated fairly. Agent Werner noted in late 1911 that the women had stopped selling their crafts at fairs because "the white people try to swindle them out of such things or try to buy them for half of what they are worth." This disillusionment with craft sales probably contributed to the hiatus in production at Southern Ute after 1911.[57] Thus, women's craft work may have provided intermittent income for a few women but it was never fully developed at Southern Ute. Women had to exploit other sources of income.

Leases on their allotments were Ute women's most frequently utilized resources. The number of leases for the entire tribe grew steadily from 1,120 in 1911 to 11,100 in 1921. While the overall amount of land was small—by 1927 Inspector H. H. Fiske calculated only 8 percent of the reservation land was leased—it represented significant activity. Out of 375 allotments, 240 had leasing enterprises at one time or another; most of them had several different leases over the first two decades of the twentieth century.[58]

The sheer number of leases precludes a detailed study of each one, but a random sampling of women's land transactions reveals some general patterns. Women were sometimes very savvy in negotiating improvements on their land. Lucy Black, for example, induced F. H. Roberts to put up a three-room house, a barn, a hog pen, and a chicken house, fence the entire allotment, and give her a cash down payment. In the opinion of one agent, "the old lady Spencer [got] an unreasonable amount of money" from the man leasing her land.[59]

Generally, however, women's land transactions were subsistence rather than entrepreneurial in nature. Single and widowed women often tried to lease their lands but were frequently forced to sell them when the leases did not work out. Agents from 1908 to 1917 carried out land transactions for at least thirty-four women. Twenty-seven of the thirty-four were widows. Of these, seventeen sold their land after failing to lease them; eleven of these seventeen widows pleaded that they must sell their lands because they had no source of income other than their annuity's money, which was inadequate for their support. Ten widows successfully leased their lands and lived off the income for a time, but seven of these leased allotments were later sold. In addition to the widows, two younger women with blind husbands leased their lands, and five young, poor, and unmarried women leased their lands before ultimately selling them. Land leasing, then, contributed to women's support throughout this era, but the leases were of short duration and frequently ended in sales.[60]

Land sales gradually alienated women — and all Utes — from a critical resource base. Mary Baker Pena noted the destructive impact of this practice in 1925. "The utes [sic] are the poorest people on earth," she wrote to the commissioner, "to save us from starving we will have to mortgage our only property." Ute land sales statistics support her contention. Out of 375 original allotments, 230 remained in Ute hands at the end of the Dawes era in 1934, that is around 33,500 acres out of the 74,100 acres originally allotted to the Indians, or approximately 46 percent.[61] While women's land transactions helped keep them from starving, they were ultimately part of a larger pattern of land alienation that contributed to tribal economic dependency and poverty.

Conclusions

The economy of the Ute reservation was impoverished throughout the Dawes period (1887–1934). The reasons for this poverty were complex and, contrary to what OIA officials thought, were not the result of Ute laziness. Ute men and women suffered deprivation, but they did not fare as badly as they perhaps could have. The Utes were never drawn into the surrounding community for menial wage work in any large numbers. They did not form an "underclass" of laborers in the mines and smelters of southern Colorado, nor did more than a handful of them perform domestic drudgery for the well-to-do families of the area. Rather, they were able to subsist on a combination of reservation wage work, subsistence agriculture and livestock raising, annuities and rations, and land leases and sales. Families shared their resources, and women's contributions of labor, rations, and money were invaluable to the tribe's survival. Despite the Office's attempts to make Indian women into homemakers supported by their husbands' wages, Ute women continued to be economically productive, challenging OIA regulations that attempted to limit their economic activities.

TWO-ROOM WOODEN HOUSE OF JULIUS CLOUD
This picture demonstrates one of the
houses of an affluent tribal leader and his wife.
*(Photograph from 1922 Industrial Report of Agent Edward E. McKean courtesy
National Archives, Rocky Mountain Region, Denver, Colorado.)*

BETSY LOPEZ AND HER LOG CABIN

Betsy looks away from the camera, her log cabin
standing in the background.

*(Photograph from 1922 Industrial Report of Agent Edward E.
McKean courtesy National Archives, Rocky Mountain Region,
Denver, Colorado.)*

ALLEN DAY SCHOOL WITH TEACHER, MRS. BESSIE ENGLISH

*(Photograph from 1922 Industrial Report of Agent Edward E. McKean courtesy
National Archives, Rocky Mountain Region, Denver, Colorado.)*

ADOBE HOUSE OF ANNIE NORRIS

This adobe home is typical of Ute homes on the reservation.

(Photograph from 1922 Industrial Report of Agent Edward E. McKean courtesy National Archives, Rocky Mountain Region, Denver, Colorado.)

CLARA BUFFALO AND CHILD

(Photograph from 1929 Industrial Report of Agent Edward E. McKean courtesy National Archives, Rocky Mountain Region, Denver, Colorado.)

SHI-RA-SA

This woman's decorated cape is an example
of Ute women's crafts.

*(Photograph from the John Wesley Powell expedition in the early
1870s courtesy Center of Southwest Studies, Fort Lewis College,
Durango, Colorado.)*

ADA B. KENT

This structure represents another kind of Ute home. Many
Utes lived at least part of the year in tents throughout the
Dawes period.

*(Photograph from 1929 Industrial Report of Agent Edward E. McKean courtesy
National Archives, Rocky Mountain Region, Denver, Colorado.)*

BUCKSKIN CHARLIE AND FAMILY

He was one of the most influential headmen of the Utes. His wife, Emma
Nailor Buck, is the woman seated farthest from him. The woman closest to
him is probably his wife's sister, A-Towee.

*(Photograph from the John Wesley Powell expedition in the early 1870s courtesy Center of
Southwest Studies, Fort Lewis College, Durango, Colorado.)*

A UTE TEPEE

Agents wanted the Utes to abandon the use of
tepees. This one was probably located in Uintah Valley, Utah.

*(Photograph from the John Wesley Powell expedition in the early 1870s courtesy Center
of Southwest Studies, Fort Lewis College, Durango, Colorado.)*

CHIEF SEVERO AND FAMILY

Another major Ute leader, Severo, stands farthest left, the man with the hat. The woman directly in front of him (not the one with the cradleboard) is his wife, Natz-chi-ve-rat.

(Photograph courtesy Center of Southwest Studies, Fort Lewis College, Durango, Colorado.)

UNIDENTIFIED UTE WOMAN WITH CHILDREN

Elimination of the "evil" cradleboard was one of the
goals of the Ute Field Matrons.

(Photograph courtesy Center of Southwest Studies, Fort Lewis College, Durango, Colorado.)

CHIPETA, WIFE OF CHIEF OURAY,
FORMAL PORTRAIT IN WASHINGTON D.C., 1880

(Photograph courtesy Center of Southwest Studies, Fort Lewis College, Durango, Colorado.)

KITTY CLOUD AND JOHN TAYLOR, WEDDING PICTURE
Kitty is marrying former slave John Taylor.
(Photograph courtesy Center of Southwest Studies, Fort Lewis College, Durango, Colorado.)

FOUR

Homemaking

In both Ute and Euro-American culture the primary gender role for women was wife and mother. Women in both cultures made a home for their families, prepared food and clothing, and cared for children. Reservation personnel, however, found Native American women's homes wanting according to middle-class, Euro-American standards of scientific housekeeping, child rearing, and consumer goods. Concerned that the lack of a "civilized" home was a major impediment to "progress," the OIA instituted a field matrons program whereby women employed by the Office went onto the reservation to train Native American women in Euro-American ideals of domesticity.[1]

Many OIA officials felt it was "futile to civilize" Indian men "so long as their women remain in ignorance and rags, and their homes and home-life riveted to their ancient barbaric habits and customs." In 1891, the Office hired three matrons "for the purpose of visiting Indian women at their homes and instructing them in domestic affairs." The program included training in "housekeeping, sewing clothes, decorating the home, and caring for animals and children." Matrons were also expected to encourage "the games and sports of white children," pressure Indian women to observe the Sabbath, urge legal marriages, and bolster Native American women's desire for consumer goods as an incentive for their husbands to work. In this manner, the OIA attacked the problem of "reactionary squaws" who retarded "progress" among Native Americans.[2]

The OIA instituted the program among the Utes in 1896 and abolished it, at least on the Ute reservation, in 1920. Eleven women served as field matrons, but only one worked before 1910. The matrons who were regular employees (not temporary) stayed on the job from one to three years. Demographic data are available for nine of the matrons. Of those, all were white and none had formal ties with religious or "Indian helper" groups. Three were widowed, one was divorced, one was single, and four were married to men in the Indian Service. Several of these women worked for the Indian Service before becoming matrons. Three came from jobs at OIA boarding schools on other reservations, two were promoted from the Southern Ute boarding school, and one had been a "housekeeper"; the others had no previous record of employment.[3] As they had done with other OIA programs, Ute women selectively appropriated certain aspects of the matrons' agenda.

Implementation of the Matrons Program at Southern Ute: Housing and Residence Patterns

The central tenet of the matrons' doctrine was efficient homemaking: "Care of a house, keeping it clean and in order, ventilated, properly warmed (not overheated), and suitably furnished[, and] adorning the home, both inside and out, with pictures, curtains, home-made rugs, flowers, grass plots and trees."[4] This home was, in OIA ideology, the foundation of "civilized" life, for policy makers believed that ideological transformation would follow changes in the material realm.

Material change was slow in coming, however. As previously noted, the Utes did not immediately embrace sedentism. Moreover, even when the Utes had homes their manner of living was far from the matrons' ideal, for many of the houses were tiny and dilapidated. Agent Edward E. McKean conducted a house-to-house survey of the reservation's eighty-three houses at the end of the Dawes period. Of the eighty-three houses, sixty-eight were two- to four-room dwellings while fifteen were one-room "shacks." The report also identified three families as tent dwellers and one who lived in a hogan.[5]

Of the sixty-six houses McKean categorized he described thirty-two as very poor, fourteen as fair, and twenty as very good. Two-thirds of the Utes, then, lived in homes that were in poor or very poor condition. Pictures accompanying the report confirm McKean's assessments. Overcrowding was also a problem, for there were three times more families than houses. The homes rated fair and very good averaged two persons per room, but eight of the homes categorized as very poor were one-room shacks averaging eight people. These averages can distort the real crowding of many of the poorest families. A number of the two-room houses held from five to seven people, and one three-room house had fourteen residents. Evaluating the subjective quality of life in these homes from the Ute point of view is difficult; since they had been accustomed to living in tepees averaging about ten feet in diameter, Ute families may not have been disturbed by these crowded conditions. Even as late as 1928, many Utes lived at least part of the year in a tepee.[6] Nevertheless, cramped housing had a disheartening effect on OIA personnel.

The ideology of the "civilizing home" was based, in part, on the privacy of the nuclear family, with separate rooms for different functions. Agent Charles Werner stated this most explicitly in 1910 when he built a model home at the Southern Ute boarding school to train the girls in housekeeping. He desired "that these girls may know the value of a separate kitchen and bedroom and insist on having the same when they secure a home of their own." He also explained that teachers trained the girls to cook individually, not collectively, so that each would learn how to prepare meals for her nuclear family once she married. The Office linked separate residences to the idea that ownership of individual property was a key "civilizing" force.[7]

For the most part, however, families at Southern Ute did not have private residences. Nuclear families lived in thirty-three houses and extended families, either multigenerational or with siblings of either the husband or the wife, occupied forty-eight houses. Married couples filled fifty-six homes, but in these households nuclear families (thirty-three) only slightly outnumbered extended (twenty-three). In the twenty-seven households without two spouses, twenty-five had extended families. Only two people lived alone.[8] The Utes seemed to utilize several residence options but the primary considerations in these choices were most likely linked to economics rather than to Anglo middle-class ideals about the family.

The majority of nuclear households on the reservation were not the prosperous homes of people who could sustain the OIA ideal of a private residence. Of the thirty-three houses containing nuclear families, McKean described only one as in "very good condition" and only eight as in "good shape." He noted that five houses were fair, three were poor, and ten were very poor. One nuclear family lived in a hogan and three lived in tents.[9] This data is somewhat surprising. While it seems logical for the poorer households to have more family members, and thus more potential income, it appears that the poorest houses on the reservation held nuclear families.

In contrast, the more prosperous families had extended households. Perhaps, then, the poorest couples could not afford to take in other family members, while those couples who had more resources continued the traditional communal ethic and shared their homes with their extended families.

The extended Ute families usually included several generations, as they had in pre-reservation times. Many men and women ages forty-six and older still had very young children or grandchildren living at home. Since agents were not always faithful about noting whether the children in the house were grandchildren, the women over fifty-six who were listed as mothers with small children were, most likely, grandmothers. This suggests that roughly half the people forty-six and over lived with their children or grandchildren, either to receive care or to help raise their grandchildren.[10]

Residence patterns also indicated something about Ute child rearing. As one goal of the matrons' program was to create "civilized mothers" to enculturate Indian children in Euro-American norms, it was important for OIA officials to isolate mothers and their offspring in nuclear families. In the extended households, relatives other than parents were available for child care and could undermine the mother's "civilizing" influence.[11] The agents' correspondence indicated that a number of Ute children were raised by persons other than their parents.

The Utes valued both motherhood and fatherhood, but they were also flexible about who carried out those roles. In many cases where one parent was absent through death or desertion the remaining parent gave the children up to relatives or friends rather than raising them alone. This pattern held for both women and men and also occasionally applied in cases of divorce. In other instances of divorce, mothers took daughters and fathers took sons. If this happened, mothers usually went to live with other relatives. In the case of orphans, if one sibling was over the age of eighteen, he or she would raise his or her younger brothers and sisters. Otherwise, the extended family or friends took the children in. Sometimes the agent was made the orphans' legal guardian.[12]

Overall, despite OIA efforts to create nuclear families, residence and child care practices continued to reflect pre-reservation patterns. Since the most prosperous Utes remained in extended families, clearly a communal ethic endured; the slight trend towards nuclear households may not have been a result of acculturation but of poverty. Ute households also continued to be multigenerational, again thwarting OIA plans to have children raised by younger more "progressive" Indians. The OIA's vision, then, was clouded by tribal actions that appeared to be both a continuation of traditional family patterns and a response to reservation indigence.

Sanitation and Disease: Infant Mortality and Women's Health Care

Pervasive poverty and disease also intruded upon the matrons' plans, requiring that they concentrate their energies on nursing, child care, and sanitation training; "care of" a home increasingly came to mean battling infant mortality and disease. For the matrons, their first line of defense in this fight was to improve sanitary conditions on the reservation.

Evaluations of sanitary conditions at Southern Ute varied from year to year and seemed dependent on the person making the report. In 1910 Agent Werner noted that Ute homes had generally been kept clean since the arrival of the field matron; in 1919 Agent Edward McKean agreed. Three separate inspectors' reports, two in 1916 and one in 1918, also praised the Utes for their cleanliness. Agents Walter Runke and Walter G. West in 1915, and Inspector W. W. McConihe in 1916, however, called Ute homes very unsanitary. Although all of these reports are vague and subjective, conflicting estimations of sanitary conditions suggest gradually improving sanitation practices. Concerns over sanitation were linked to reducing infant mortality — a primary preoccupation of the matrons. Thus, the matrons' activities were often the focal point of either praise or blame in these appraisals.[13]

The 1910 and 1911 annual reports of Agent Charles Werner commended matrons Lizzie McCorquordale and Cora Hutchinson for decreasing the number of infant deaths by improving Ute housekeeping. The reports gave no specific examples of what the matrons did. Twenty-three babies were born in 1911, at the time of a smallpox epidemic; seven of them died but Werner credited Hutchinson with saving the other sixteen. Throughout 1914 and 1915, during the tenure of Martha Morris, the problems continued. Eight out of fourteen infants died in 1914 during a typhoid epidemic; seven out of twelve babies died in 1915. In 1916 the OIA launched the "Save the Babies" campaign nationwide. The crusade consisted of education in hygiene and home sanitation, increased prenatal care and doctors' or matrons' attendance at births, postnatal classes (emphasizing bottle feeding) and "clean and healthy baby" contests — offering prizes for the baby kept the cleanest from May through July 15. A committee of three Indian women, under the direction of Matron Morris, conducted the classes and judged the babies for the contest.[14]

During this campaign, Morris drew both criticism and praise for her efforts. Agency physician Paul Capps reproached her for not being diligent enough in sanitation work. Inspector Newburne, in 1916, did not meet

Morris but noted that she assisted with four of the seven births that year —
during which only one baby died. Agent West also praised Morris's work,
blaming infant deaths on the lack of a reservation hospital. In contrast,
Home Economics supervisor Elsie Newton, in 1915, described Morris as
"a well-intentioned, conscientious, person, neat, presentable, kindly, but
[who] lacks force [and] has not [a] definite program of work." Inspector
W. W. McConihe met Morris in 1916 and concluded she was "lacking in
aggressiveness and positiveness and also in initiative." He observed that
her lectures on child care and hygiene were not given in Ute women's
homes but were only delivered on ration days when the Indians came to the
agency. Further, McConihe noted that Ute women seemed to "resent [her]
interference in their mode of living or the conduct of their affairs." Morris
herself had a very negative attitude toward Ute women, complaining that
they were lazy and had no ambition. Her condescending feelings may account for what several observers saw as her lack of success.[15]

Nevertheless, the "Save the Babies" contests of 1916–19 represented an
area of limited cooperation between Ute women and matrons. Eighteen
women participated in the contest; with 120 families allegedly living in
permanent houses, the level of cooperation seems unimpressive. All of the
women who took part in the contest, however, were between the ages of
eighteen and thirty-five. Some of these women may have been either pregnant or the mothers of the seven children born in 1916.[16]

Although the women's motivation for entering this contest is not documented in the records, it is possible to speculate. Participation may suggest
some level of assimilation. Exposure to the educational system may have
been relevant, for twelve of these women were in their twenties and had
attended OIA schools. On the other hand, the women's actions may not
reflect a greater degree of assimilation. Given the high infant mortality
rate, desperation may have pressed some mothers to attend. Others may
have come out of curiosity, a desire to win the prizes, or a need to socialize.
Whatever their reasons, Agent West was confident that their cooperation
with the matron would lower the infant mortality rate.[17]

In 1917, efforts to reduce infant mortality continued with a program
known as "Baby Week." Matron Josephine Belt set up exhibits in her quarters and invited Ute women to view them. Among the articles were baby
clothes, baby and toddler food, a crib with a fly screen, a playpen, and items
"unsuitable for children" including pacifiers, "cheap candy," coffee, pickles,
and gum. Demonstrations of how to milk a cow, use fly traps, bathe babies,
and give infants boiled water to drink were juxtaposed with lectures showing improper baby care, especially using cradle boards and, in a reversal of

the previous year's instructions, bottle feeding. About sixty Utes, male and female, and twenty children, from infancy to four years old, viewed the presentations.[18]

Agent West's interpretation of "Baby Week" was ambivalent. He noted that "difficulty was experienced in getting the Indians to participate" but also concluded that "progress had been made" and that infants were surviving in increasing numbers. An OIA inspector following up the contest in 1918 believed that the death rate for infants was indeed dropping. Yet in 1918 four out of nine babies died, and in 1919 five out of seven died; influenza epidemics accounted for these high numbers. In 1922, after the OIA abolished the position of matron for the Ute reservation, Inspector John Atwater expressed concern that the Ute population was again declining. By 1922, the population of Southern Utes was down to 329. The population had remained in the high 360s throughout the previous decade, and Atwater felt that the lack of a matron was at least partially responsible for the health problems on the reservation.[19]

The causal connection between declining infant death rates and matrons' activities cannot be established with certainty. Nevertheless, demographic data demonstrates that infant deaths had fallen by half by the end of the period in which the matrons worked (1910–20). Even with the influenza epidemics during 1918 and 1919, infant deaths declined from thirty-three during the period 1910–15 to fourteen during the period 1915–20 (see table 4.1).[20] The matrons may have been a significant variable in this trend, for their presence seems to have encouraged Ute women to seek medical care, including assistance with childbirth.

Before the arrival of the matrons, women rarely sought medical help from reservation doctors. In 1897, the agency physician, speaking of his efforts to fight venereal disease, claimed that Ute men "come and are treated willingly but the women are mean and stubborn and some of them say that they will rather die than be treated." Statistical evidence indicates that Ute women were initially significantly more conservative about health care than were men but that they gradually grew more willing to receive care after the arrival of the matrons (see table 4.2).[21]

Perusal of the matrons' reports indicates that Ute women frequently made use of matron nursing services. Lizzie McCorquordale, matron for several months in 1910, took medicine to sick Indian women and cleaned their houses, cared for women's wounds and "diseased skin," rheumatism, "sore eyes," tonsillitis, tuberculosis, and "other ailments." She also gave vaccinations to Indian children. Mellie Martin, matron from 1911 to 1913, noted caring for women and children with trachoma, smallpox, sore eyes,

Table 4.1
Infant Deaths Among the Utes, 1911–25

Year	Births	Deaths	Infant Deaths	Total Population
1911	23	13	7	362
1912	17	6	5	367
1913	8	15	6	360
1914	14	24	8	—
1915	12	10	7	366
1916	7	8	1	365
1917	18	14	3	372
1918	9	16	4	369
1919	7	42	5	341
1920	12	11	1	334
1922	12	4	3	329
1923	—	—	—	—
1924	—	—	—	—
1925	28	26	7	—

Source: *ARCIA*, 1911–25.

scrofula, gonorrhea, and syphilis, and concluded that she found "many afflicted with different complications [and] in need of a doctor." Between January of 1913 and January of 1914, Cora Hutchinson nursed tuberculosis, sore eyes, trachoma, and venereal disease. Martha Morris, matron from 1914 to 1917, affirmed that she treated sick Indians but gave no details as to their illnesses. Josephine Belt, matron from 1917 to 1919, also claimed to have logged many miles providing nursing, prenatal care, delivering babies, and caring for Mary Buck, "she being insane." She spoke of how women came to her house and took her with them to nurse their sick friends and family. "I have not only set [sic] up one night with sick Indians but many," she declared.[22]

The matrons appear to have brought Ute women into the Indian Service health care system because of the Utes' preferences and the matrons' initiative. First, women were often the healers in traditional Ute culture. Ute shamans were both male and female, but herbalists, who specialized in curing disease, were almost always female. Ute women probably used male shamans at times, but they were accustomed to accepting medical aid from other women. Second, the matrons visited women in their homes, thus increasing the opportunities for women to get medical attention. Dr. Blachly commented in 1890 that the majority of Indians he saw were those who

Table 4.2
Doctors' Visits to Utes, by Gender

Year	Ute Population Males	Females
1880[a]	243	208
1900[b]	106	140
1912	104	102
1923	99	99
1932	108	109

Year	Doctors' Visits Males	Females
1881–85	1,032	625
1886–90	3,948	1,692
1891–95	1,688	1,364[c]
1904–09	2,406	1824
1911–14	330	369
1916–18	456	431
1919–21	297	201
1923–25	525	475[d]

Sources: For the Ute population: Census Summary, 1880, 1900, 1912, 1923, 1932, Southern Ute Census Records, Stewart Collection; for the doctors' visits: Monthly Sanitary Reports, 1879–94, and Quarterly Sanitary Reports, 1895–1909, RCUA, 44103, boxes 155–56; *SANR*, 1911–18, RCUA, 44016, boxes 7 and 8.
[a]No breakdown by age is available.
[b]Males over eighteen; females over fourteen.
[c]High figures in these years reflect epidemics of bronchitis during the period 1886–88, conjunctivitis in 1887, influenza in 1891, and catarrh in 1892.
[d]The 1923–25 figures include the Weminuches.

lived near the agency and who came to him. The Indians residing farther away from his office did not send for him, and he rarely visited them on his own initiative. Until 1921, succeeding doctors also depended on the Utes coming to the agency for attention.[23]

During most of the Dawes years, women and children's health care was conducted almost entirely at home or in a matron's quarters. Mercy Hospital in nearby Durango, Colorado, took some Ute patients in emergency cases. Most Ute men used the agency physician; women saw the matrons and, later, the field service nurses who were phased into the Indian service as the matrons' program declined in the mid-1920s. Women's health issues

were key in the pleas of agents and inspectors for a hospital at Southern
Ute. Agent Werner, in 1909, Agent West, in 1914, and agency physicians
Robbins (1909) and Capps (1914) claimed that the Utes themselves had
requested a hospital. This appeal was finally granted in 1930 and 1931,
when the OIA constructed hospitals at Ute Mountain and Southern Ute
respectively. The reports of field nurses from the years 1929–34 indicate
that the majority of Southern Ute women sought prenatal care and, after
1931, had their children in the hospital. Gradually, Ute women became
willing to see the agency physician. Carl Lefforge, who had served as doctor
since 1921, reported that for many years, Ute women rarely called him for
"confinement"; by 1930, however, he recorded, "I am called in by most
of them."[24] By the end of the Dawes period, then, Ute women appeared to
be actively seeking assistance with both illness and childbirth, and infant
deaths had declined.

Homemaking and the Decorative Arts: Domesticity

The officials who designed the matrons program never intended the matrons to spend all of their time dispensing medical aid; rather they were
meant to impart middle-class respectability to Indian women. The ideology of "uplift" naively assumed that providing a house and "proper" furnishings would automatically "incite among Indians generally aspirations
for improvement in their life — morally, intellectually, socially, and reli-
giously."[25] While caring for the sick may have absorbed much of the matrons' time and energy, they still tried to teach Indian women how to create
a home decorated and furnished according to Euro-American standards
and equipped with modern homemaking technology.

Ornamental skills taught by matrons included rug making, crocheting,
picture and wallpaper hanging, and embroidery. These activities may appear frivolous in the face of reservation impoverishment, but they were
important to the matrons inasmuch as their conceptions of a "home" included such niceties. As in other areas of matrons' activities, Ute women
selectively cooperated with this agenda.

Matrons' reports document attempts to teach Ute women Euro-
American ornamental skills, even when they still lived in tepees. In 1910
Lizzie McCorquordale visited Indian families residing in both houses and
tepees, making curtains for one family and teaching the wife "how to hang
and drape them," and hanging paper in one of the houses. She endeavored
"to instill a desire for nice things" in the women by teaching embroidery

and quilting, and by planting flowers at her cottage. Mellie Martin, the next matron, mentioned that Ute women attended sewing classes at her quarters. Cora Hutchinson, a temporary matron for four months in 1913, taught fifteen women sewing and "domestic economy" and held sewing classes attended by "several" Ute women. Her successor, Martha Morris, taught baking and sewing to "several families." Between 1917 to 1919, Josephine Belt told of giving sewing classes at her home (sharing her patterns in order to teach the women "to economize") and of teaching knitting, crocheting, tatting, braiding rugs, cooking, canning, and making of baby layettes (clothing, diapers, blankets)—also in her home, as "Indian women and girls are here every day."[26]

Those who observed Belt's work commented on her good rapport with the Utes. Special Inspector Horace G. Wilson praised her as "one of the most efficient, hard-working, Field Matrons in the Indian Service." Superintendent McKean claimed that Belt's personality and tact gave her a "natural ability" to gain the Indians' confidence, and Inspector L. F. Michael also noted that the Utes told him Belt was well liked.[27] Belt offered more classes in cooking and sewing than any other matron. Communal sewing and cooking were activities that Ute women had shared with Anglo women before their confinement to the reservation. The sessions offered at the matrons' quarters provided a familiar form of fellowship and task sharing that the women seemed to enjoy.[28]

Belt's records contain clues as to why Ute women may have attended matrons' classes. During her classes, Belt fed the women food she prepared from government supplies. She also provided them with sewing and cooking materials: "There is not a day but some Indians are here for some errand or other . . . patterns, medicine, or some other necessity and I have never refused an Indian any thing I have."[29] While Ute women may have sincerely desired training in both cooking and sewing, free food and fellowship may also have motivated them to visit these classes.

Further, many of these sessions were devoted to preparing fair exhibits. One of the most popular activities on the reservation was the Southern Ute Fair. The Ute always enthusiastically supported the fairs, which had been established before the matrons arrived. Although men's categories always outnumbered women's (and paid better premiums), the exhibits in the "Domestic Department" were also popular. Describing the first fair, held in 1907, Agent Charles Werner commented, "A baby show was a very amusing feature, a premium being offered for the healthiest and cleanest baby. Every child whom they thought had a chance was brought in." The baby contest continued to be a favorite over the years.[30]

Some stalls at the fair showcased women's native craft skills, such as the display of bead work and moccasins; others rewarded Euro-American work. Ute judges awarded prizes for the best bread, pie, cake, and machine sewing and, to emphasize individualism in domestic tasks, the highest prizes ($2.50 for first prize) went to "best display of hand sewing made by one person" and "best display of cooking done by one person."[31]

Why did the Utes embrace the fair with such interest? Perhaps it was because it was an occasion to exert a modicum of Indian autonomy. Agent Werner first proposed the fair in 1907, but he let the Utes take almost complete charge of organizing it and judging the entries. "The Indians seemed proud that this fair was all their own," he wrote, "and have talked about it a great deal since." Seven years later, the enthusiasm still ran high for the fair as "practically all the Indians of this jurisdiction met in council and selected a committee to act in furthering the fair." The Utes raised all the premium monies, initially from their own funds but later from the sales of concessions, private subscribers, and gate receipts.[32]

Another reason for the fair's popularity may have been connected with its celebration of traditional native crafts and activities, such as racing and shooting arrows. Many Utes turned out for the occasion in "buckskin suits, war bonnets, dance costumes, Navajo blankets and jewelry; to put it mild [sic] there was never a grander display in that line." Ute women displayed their babies for the baby contest in handmade beaded buckskin attire. Tepees, clothing, baskets, cradle boards, and carved wooden utensils were all places where Ute women with an artistic bent could paint, bead, fringe, and embroider with porcupine quills. Southern Ute women were known for their excellent bead work.[33] The sewing contests represented a place where Ute women could continue their traditional needlework skills in new materials, and sometimes with new technology.

The Utes may also have found the fair's prizes to be an incentive to participate. While premiums at the fairs were low, for the poorest Indians, $2.50 prize money may have been important. Some years, the agency ran contests offering significant prizes. In 1917, inspired by the success of the fairs, the agency ran an Adult Industrial Contest that offered a sewing machine as first prize and a washing machine as second, for the most industrious Indian family. Agents selected winners on the basis of points given for evidence of "progressive" activities such as a clean home, the best garden or crops, etc. The agency farmers and field matrons graded contestants in daily reports.[34] There are no records of how many Utes entered this particular contest, but given the prizes, participation may have been fairly high, for Ute women were enthusiastic about Euro-American homemaking goods and technology.

Labor-saving technology appealed to Ute women. In 1880, long before most Utes lived in houses, Agent Henry Page ordered 250 "small size cast iron bake ovens [because some Utes] have procured old bake ovens from settlers and nearly all would gladly use them could they obtain them." Agent Charles A. Bartholomew ordered the reservation's first sewing machine in 1892. The agency trader gave lessons on the machine to "a number" of Ute women in 1895. Describing the scene, one observer wrote that the women "grasped the idea readily, and soon were able to make garments." "Of course the trader has an eye to the main chance," he noted, "He realizes that the more the women can sew, the more dresses they will want." Ute women were quick to see the advantages of sewing machines. In 1910 Louisa Poor Washington, who was living in a tent, ordered a machine for $40 and a new tent for $25. In his letter approving this purchase, Agent Charles Werner noted that while most of the Utes lived in tents, especially in the summer, "Many of the Indian women have learned to use a machine in making their clothes."[35] OIA personnel were pleased to see such "progress."

Policy makers stressed that material prosperity was an essential component of the "civilizing" ideology, both in creating the ambiance of "civilization" and in providing motivation for the work ethic. Continual emphasis on consumer goods by both matrons and agents gradually encouraged the Utes to appropriate more household items. In 1916 Agent Walter West built fifty dining tables and benches. He also planned to build cupboards and beds and purchase dishes and stoves for all the houses. In 1918 Agent Edward McKean reported that the field matron persuaded many Utes to "fix up" their houses with paint, paper, and curtains and to "spend considerable portions" of their money on dishes, bedding, and utensils as they were "becoming more eager to acquire things." He noted that eight homes had sewing machines and thirteen were "well-furnished." By 1929 he described thirty-five of the seventy-five inhabited houses as "well-furnished." While fewer than half of the Indian dwellings had beds, tables, chairs, and stoves by 1929, Agent McKean was satisfied by the Utes' acquisition of dry goods.[36] Outside observers despaired, however, that adoption of these items had not instilled a Euro-American homemaking ethic based on "scientific housekeeping."

Two OIA inspectors in 1929 and 1931 evaluated the results of homemaking programs at Southern Ute. Supervisor of Indian Industries Charles E. Farin, in 1929, noted that "a large number of Utes have fair homes — [the]

condition of which is the problem. New floors, window panes, door panels, wallboard or plaster, [and] paint are needed in every home." Farin felt that Ute women needed "a new interest [and] better sanitation" in their homes. In 1931 Inspector G. E. E. Lindquist was also unhappy with what he viewed as the "squalor" of Ute homes. "Among the Southern Ute," he wrote, "there is no lack of houses, such as they are, but rather [the need is for an] infusing of a new spirit into homemaking." He alleged that Ute women neglected housekeeping tasks in order to gamble. At the OIA's request, Rosemary Trant, teacher of Home Economics for the Ute Mountain boarding school, visited Ute homes in 1931 attempting to "improve" Ute women's homemaking skills.[37]

The OIA inspectors blamed disinterested Ute women for the poor conditions of Ute homes, but Trant remarked that the women seemed responsive to her efforts to teach them better housekeeping. Thus, evaluation of the attempt to impose "scientific housekeeping" on Ute women is difficult. Since sanitation practices seemed to be improving, and since disease and infant mortality fell, the matrons and, later, the field nurses and home economics teachers probably had some effect on housekeeping. Furthermore, the Utes had adopted houses, for at least part of the year, and acquired furnishings and other household items. While these houses and furnishings seemed poor to the OIA inspectors, to the agents who lived amidst the reservation poverty these things were evidence of "progress." The inspectors' evaluations may simply reflect their desire to see a middle-class standard of living that was difficult for Ute women to obtain. Finally, it is impossible to discern whether Indian women consciously resisted the OIA's homemaking agenda, or desired more material prosperity but were deterred by poverty.[38]

Conclusions

The matrons program was founded in the 1880s on the perception that "the non progressive ideas of women [were] the greatest bar to Indian advancement" and that the remedy for this condition was "the regeneration of the race through the women."[39] The OIA hoped to create a "civilizing" home — a middle-class nuclear family home reflecting the "uplifting" virtues of domesticity. Over time, however, the matrons focused more on issues of public health, such as sanitation and health care, until they were eventually replaced by a corps of field nurses. From the beginning, no OIA administrator acknowledged the limitations that reservation poverty placed on their vision. Office personnel blamed the setbacks and failures of the program on Ute women, whom they viewed as lazy or indifferent to their "proper" domestic role.

Although Ute women joined with Ute men in resisting sedentism, they were not the hopeless reactionaries of some OIA rhetoric, at least not with respect to the matrons. Rather, Ute women responded to the matrons' activities by selective borrowing. They appear to have embraced some of the matrons' ideas about sanitation, health care, home furnishings, and homemaking technology; yet they received the matrons on Ute terms, accepting them in traditional female roles as healers and midwives (before eventually embracing male doctors), and also continuing pre-reservation communal work patterns in homemaking tasks. As a result of Ute women's limited cooperation with the matrons' program, infant deaths fell significantly during the matron years. Nevertheless, by the end of the Dawes period Ute women still did not have the middle-class homes of the reformers' vision. The OIA domestic vision, like a gendered economy, required a level of prosperity unobtainable on the reservation. If the OIA could not transform Ute homes according to Euro-American ideals, the failure was most likely due to economic conditions rather than women's resistance.

FIVE

Sex and Marriage

As part of their restructuring of native cultures, the OIA attempted to force Indians to confine their sexual activity to permanent, monogamous marriages — preferably state-sanctioned (although for the purpose of determining heirs, the OIA recognized tribal marriages for Indians "prior to allotment").[1] Agents intruded into Indian sexual and marital choices in a number of ways. They tried to force men and women caught in premarital sexual activity to marry, they pressured couples married by tribal custom to "legitimize" their unions, and they attempted to return "runaway" wives. They also occasionally made decisions about who was an acceptable partner for an individual Ute and who could marry whom on the reservation. In several instances, agents broke up unions they deemed unsuitable. The agents were also responsible for enforcing laws regulating sexual morality. In carrying out these activities, OIA personnel applied both exhortation and sanction.

The extent to which agents were able to change the Utes' sexual behavior, however, is questionable. Many Utes appeared to make their own choices about sexual activity: couples declined to marry when caught in premarital sexual activity, women frequently refused to stay in bad marriages, and a number of couples resisted the pressure to "legitimize" their unions, even when faced with penalties against their children. While the number of legal nuptials rose during this period, there is also evidence that Utes married and divorced according to tribal custom without the agents' knowledge. As in other areas, assimilationist policy brought about superficial modifications in Ute behavior, but on a deeper level the Utes shaped their own destiny as much as they could.

Perceptions of Sexual Propriety

OIA personnel encouraged Indians to abstain from sex outside of marriage and to marry and divorce according to the laws of the state, and the Office drafted guidelines regulating Indian marriages. The *Rulebook for the Court of Indian Offenses*, published in 1883, authorized punishments for certain sexual and marital transgressions. Interestingly, these rules often focused on the behavior of Indian men. The *Rulebook* declared polygamy to be a crime, imposing a fine and twenty days at hard labor on the offending male and withholding rations from him until he dissolved his illegal union(s), presumably keeping the first wife. It also noted that any man who "fail[ed], without cause, to support his wife and children" would not be issued any rations until he proved to the court that he would provide for his family. Finally, any Indian or mixed-blood man who offered to pay an Indian family "to cohabit with a girl or woman of the family" lost his rations and could spend up to sixty days in jail. The same penalty held for the family member who took the money. This person could, presumably, be either male or female, and the *Rulebook* made no gender distinctions regarding chastisement for this particular offense. Nevertheless, overall, the punishments prescribed by the book focused on Indian men, implying that they were lustful and irresponsible and would seduce and abandon women and not support their children.[2]

Although official policies regarding sex and marriage mentioned only Indian men, OIA personnel on reservations and in boarding schools often concentrated most of their "moral uplift" activities on women. The ideology of women's purity informed the OIA focus on women as agents of change in sexual matters. According to nineteenth-century prescriptive literature, women were naturally "passionless" and sexually pure. The conviction that women were morally superior to men underscored OIA attempts to change Native Americans' sexual behavior. Addressing a convention of Indian school workers in 1900, Cora Dunn, superintendent of the Rainy Mountain School of Anadarko, Oklahoma, advocated "the regeneration of the race through the women," for if the Office "improved" the morals of women, "the men w[ould] follow." The OIA's instructions to the field matrons echoed this opinion. Matrons were to encourage Native American women to keep their marriage vows and teach them to organize "societies for promoting literary, religious, moral, and social improvement." In this way, Indian women could "refine" their people's morality.[3]

Enforcement of this policy reflected many tensions and ambiguities, however. Although some policy makers argued that women were the key to moral uplift, others doubted Indian women's ability to adhere to Euro-American sexual morality. On the Southern Ute reservation, exhortations were accompanied by coercive measures designed to force Ute women to comply with OIA norms or to compel them into pressuring their husbands into compliance. Some OIA personnel treated Ute women as sexual predators. Moreover, a double standard prevailed in punishment and policy enforcement. In instances where agents discovered premarital or extramarital relations, the women suffered sanctions for penalties misconduct more frequently than did the men. Thus, the agents did not trust Ute women's innate purity, but rather treated them as "loose women" who must be constrained and punished before Ute morals could "improve." This view implied that some OIA personnel believed that women's supposed moral superiority appertained only with white women.[4]

Further, enforcement of policy was not consistent. Some agents, most notably William D. Leonard (1906–7) and Charles F. Werner (1907–12), were quite zealous in policing Ute morals. Others, such as David A. Day (1894–97), Charles E. McChesney (1913), Walter G. West (1915–17), and Edward E. McKean (1918–26), appeared less enthusiastic but still tried to promote the OIA moral agenda. One agent, however, came under severe criticism for failing to regulate Ute sexual conduct. Some agency employees and outside observers accused Edward Peacore (1930–32) of allowing rampant sexual misconduct at the agency because he himself engaged in extramarital sex with an OIA employee.

Indian men also occasionally tried to control the sexual behavior of Ute women. Several Ute men (and one non-Ute husband of a Ute woman) called on agents to force their "runaway" wives to return to them. Most of the time the agents agreed that the absent wives must be brought back to their husbands. In short, while some Ute men and OIA personnel were sometimes in conflict over sexual concerns, others of them joined forces to attempt control over Ute women.

Agents' views on sexual morality at Southern Ute varied. In 1877, upon meeting the Utes for the first time, Agent Francis Weaver commented, "There is but a single feature in their character which, if I am correctly informed, is to be admired, and that is that they are exceedingly chaste." In 1890 Agent Charles Bartholomew echoed Weaver's sentiment, writing, "The reputation of the Southern Ute women for morality ranks with the best of any tribe with which I have had acquaintance." In 1913 Agent Stephen Abbot credited the Utes with regarding marriage ties as sacred.

Other agents' opinions about Ute morals, however, were more negative. In 1893 Agent H. B. Freeman lamented the pattern of continually shifting marriages at Southern Ute. David A. Day commented in 1894, "Immorality prevails among them to an extent rendering loathsome diseases quite common." William D. Leonard, who supervised the agency from 1906 to 1907, was one of the most virulent critics of Ute morals; his annual reports contained numerous disparaging remarks on Ute sexual morality.[5]

In fact, Ute ideas on sex and marriage did not radically differ from Euro-American ones. The Utes discouraged premarital sexual activity but were realistic about the likelihood of young people abstaining. Consequently, there were no sanctions brought against couples who had sex before they were married. Two people intent on becoming permanent partners would call each other *piwan'na'pun*, meaning sweetheart, and they were then officially engaged. The Utes viewed the engagement period as a "trial marriage." Although their parents protested that they should not, engaged couples usually had sexual intercourse. If the pair proved compatible, the woman's mother made her daughter's lover a tepee, and the two began living together as husband and wife.[6]

Ute couples sometimes had a marriage ceremony, the smoke-test ordeal. The ceremony was not required and was performed as a part of the trial marriage in order to help determine compatibility. In this ritual, an engaged couple was confined for several hours in a smoke-filled tepee, where they had to remain courteous to one another. If the man and women argued during this test or if they fainted, their families judged them to be incompatible and urged them to separate. Any couple who passed the trial but later found they could not live together, simply parted. The Utes also occasionally practiced polygyny.[7]

Egalitarian gender relationships prevailed in sex and marriage. Decisions about sexual activity were up to the individual — men had no control over women's sexual behavior either before or after marriage. Families could not compel a woman to marry or remain in a marriage, but social custom encouraged both men and women to heed their parents' advice. If a woman was caught in adultery, her husband usually demanded some form of restitution from her lover, but he did not punish her. A woman who discovered her husband's extramarital affair could fight her rival for her spouse or she could give her husband over to the other woman and then destroy that woman's personal belongings as compensation. Women who desired a divorce could either leave or ask their husbands to leave. Men were also free to leave unhappy marriages. In short, individuals — men and women — had control over their own sexual behavior in Ute culture.[8]

Premarital Sex, Extramarital Sex, and Women's Autonomy

As previously mentioned, OIA personnel sought to regulate Indians' sexuality, and women became a focus of the campaign. In 1912 Superintendent Frederick Snyder of the Santa Fe Indian school learned that U. W., a Southern Ute student, was about four months pregnant. Snyder promptly informed Ute agent Charles McChesney. His letter reflects the double standard agents sometimes used in dealing with violations of Euro-American sexual mores. "Jay B., one of the boys who came with the party last fall, brought this trouble to her," he wrote, "now she should be expelled, but what about him? Should he come home and marry her?"[9] U. W.'s expulsion from school was considered automatic but Jay's was a matter of question.

McChesney replied that Snyder should return both parties to the reservation. U. W. gave birth to a boy named Randolph. The couple were wed but theirs is the only case on record where a couple discovered in premarital sexual activity married. Jay and U. W. appear in the 1923 census as husband and wife along with their four children. Evidently their relationship was not a casual one, for they were still married in 1932.[10] The couple's devotion to one another probably accounts for the agent's success in compelling them to marry. In all other cases where couples were caught in sexual activity, the agents failed to link the pair in matrimony.

No agent forced A. B. to marry, although she conceived a child out of wedlock. A. B. attended Southern Ute boarding school. When she was fifteen years old, the principal teacher at the school whipped her with a garden hose for "persisting in writing notes to certain large boys." The report does not mention whether or not the recipients of the notes responded or if they were also punished.[11] A. B. transferred to the Santa Fe Indian school in 1917 where, early in October, she wrote to Agent Edward McKean complaining of homesickness.

> Us Ute girls always think of home and sometimes we get hungry, and also that I want to ask you if you could send us some money. We want to by coats and trunks. . . . We only have suitcases and these girls get into it and take our stamps and some of money out if you send us $15.00. Its so cold down here. Yesterday morning the wind was blowing forces when we were going to breakfast. I hope to hear from you all.

McKean replied to A. B.'s letter by sending her money, assuring her that her loneliness would be over soon, and telling her that she and her friends should "stay at school and be good girls."[12]

Two months later A. B. again wrote of her unhappiness at school and requested money to return home.

we don't like to stay here because the girls steal everything from us our stamps and writing paper. We cannot get along with them. Some of the girls are very nice and I know its a very nice place and its getting cold and some of the girls are catching very bad colds. You must send money for us. Please. We want to go back home.

McKean never replied.[13]

Within three months Santa Fe superintendent Snyder informed McKean that A. B. was "in a family way" and would have to be returned to the Ute reservation. A. B. named Tim T. as the father, apparently confessing that "the trouble happened at home before she came here to school." Tim T., aged nineteen, appears on the 1912 Ute census and then disappears from the records. Despite pressures from Agent McKean, A. B. did not marry Tim. Rather, she took a job working for wages near Southern Ute and lived with her mother.[14] She worked from 1917 until 1919 when she died during a flu epidemic. Papers from her inheritance hearing, inexplicably not held until 1927, recorded that the only heir was her child, "the son of the deceased Herbert M." The boy lived with A. B.'s mother.[15]

Agency records do not indicate that A. B. ever married. Who, then, was Herbert M.? Herbert M. was Hispanic and appears nowhere in Ute agency records. Was he the child's real father or did the M. family adopt him because of some connection with A. B.'s family? It was not uncommon for Hispanic families near the reservation to adopt Ute children who worked for them as laborers. Perhaps A. B.'s son worked for the M. family while he was living with his grandmother. In any case, rather than assuming a homemaker role, A. B. found employment and no one forced her to marry either man.

In 1915, when A. B. was whipped for being a flirt, two other young Ute women were also whipped for expressing "inappropriate" interest in young men. Southern Ute boarding school teachers beat E. T. (sixteen years old) and F. S. (also sixteen) "for entering the quarters of the boys after bed time." Upon learning of this action, Agent Walter G. West noted that he disapproved of corporal punishment but recognized the necessity for "drastic measures to prevent grave offenses." Again, there is no mention of whipping the boys as well.[16] Examination of both women's lives illuminates the tensions between agents and young Ute women over appropriate conduct for Ute women.

E. T.'s whipping for contact with "boys" in 1915 was not her first. While attending the Allen day school on the reservation in 1913, headmaster Joseph D. Turner discovered E. T. (then fourteen) "meeting with one of the boys, twice, to our knowledge," and beat her. After the punishment she ran away to live with her mother, K. T. Headmaster Turner informed Agent Stephen Abbot that, in consideration of the other children, he would not allow E. T. to return to the day school. He suggested she be sent to a boarding school.[17]

After the 1915 incident at the boy's dorm, Agent West sent E. T. to the Santa Fe Indian school. In 1916 she turned up pregnant and had to be sent home. Her father, John T., cautioned against sending E. T.'s mother to get her and suggested that field matron Martha Morris escort his daughter home. He also refused to reimburse the agency for the two women's trip and told West to deduct the expenses from E. T.'s money. Sending Morris after E. T., West apologized to Superintendent Snyder for E. T.'s condition and vowed to find out who the baby's father was so that he could "protect her interests" as well as he could by persuading the couple to marry.[18]

E. T. had a daughter in 1916 and named her Frances. The 1923 census records her as the head of her house with Frances, Ruby, born in 1918, and John, born in 1923. Like A. B., E. T. did not have a "shotgun wedding" but rather set up her own household and raised her children for a time without a man in the house. Later she married her third child's father, and she appears in the 1930 Ute census as E. T. V. — married.[19]

Officials at the Santa Fe school also returned F. S. (also whipped for sneaking into the boys' dorms at the Ute boarding school) to the Ute reservation for sexual misconduct, although records do not state specifically what she did. Agent West noted in 1916 that F. S. had once been "considered a very good girl, but a short time before she went to Santa Fe she began to show a disposition to be wild and irresponsible." He hesitated to allow her back into school for fear she would be a "bad example" to the other girls there.[20]

F. S. then applied for admission to the Sherman Institute at Riverside, California, in 1918. John D. De Huff of the Santa Fe school, had to explain to the CIA how F. S. "loved not wisely but too well; I am not able to ascertain from the correspondence on file here whether the young woman became pregnant or not." The OIA recommended that Superintendent F. M. Conser of the Sherman Institute check on F. S.'s actions since her earlier "immoral conduct" and determine if she was "trying to live the right kind of life." If she were, she should be admitted to the school, provided that she was no older than twenty-one.[21] F. S. disappears from the records after this letter.

F. S.'s situation differed from that of the other women in one important way: Agent West viewed her experience as statutory rape. "It may interest you to know," he wrote to Snyder in 1917, "that I have had a Mexican 'jugged' for his conduct with F. S. . . . and the specific charge is statutory rape which the fellow admits."[22] The agency records contain no documents of this man's trial, and without his name he cannot be traced in the court records. His fate, then, is uncertain but his arrest raises a number of interesting questions.

Why did West arrest F. S.'s lover for rape? None of the other men was arrested for engaging in sexual contact with these schoolgirls. F. S.'s age was not the primary concern — all of the women caught in sexual misconduct were under the age of eighteen and were, according to Colorado statute law, minors. Colorado law also defined as rape any sexual contact — consensual or nonconsensual — between any man over the age of fourteen and any woman under the age of eighteen.[23] Legally, then, any man in any one of these relationships could have been charged with rape. While it is possible that a rape occurred, there is nothing in the records to indicate that F. S. viewed her experiences this way. Why was this man charged?

Agent West was not enforcing anti-miscegenation laws. As late as 1935, Colorado law prohibited intermarriage between whites and "Negroes or mulattoes [sic]" but there was no law prohibiting marriage between whites and Hispanics. The law specifically allowed "people living in that portion of the state acquired from Mexico" (the area including the reservation) to marry "according to the custom of that country." Racism may still have played a role in the man's arrest. Agency records contain frequent references to "low Mexicans" who corrupted the Utes with sexual promiscuity and liquor. In his annual reports of 1915–17, West made derogatory comments about "Mexican" bootleggers who supplied the Utes with liquor.[24] He apparently viewed F. S.'s sexual contact with a Hispanic man as evidence of male aggression.

On the other hand, reservation personnel also viewed these particular Ute women as sexual aggressors. Before their expulsion from boarding school, OIA teachers beat A. B., E. T., and F. S. for interacting with Ute men in a way suggesting sexual interest; the men, as objects of this interest, escaped punishment. The "double standard" applied to punishment of sexual activity indicated that agents sometimes regarded Ute women as sexual predators preying on men. That the only man to be punished for sex with one of these women was Hispanic reinforces this view. As arbitrators of reservation sexual morality, OIA agents punished Ute women for expressing lascivious desires, yet they also felt the women needed protection from the lust of nearby Hispanic men. Agents felt an obligation to protect any children resulting from premarital sexual activity as well.

In each case where premarital sexual contact resulted in pregnancy, the agents insisted — though not always successfully — on immediate legal marriage. Attempts to force sexually active couples into matrimony were most likely motivated by concepts of children's legitimacy, which was always an OIA concern. Agents tied illegitimacy to the larger question of marital stability, which they in turn linked to their campaign to replace marriage by tribal custom with state-sanctioned marriages.

Because OIA policy declared lawful unions to be more "stable" than marriages by tribal custom, Ute agents promoted lawful marriages among the Utes. Some agents employed the threat of punishments for "unlawful cohabitation," more specifically for women and children of such couplings. William D. Leonard, agent in 1906 and 1907, played on the idea that Ute women were dependent on their husbands' support and could be used to pressure men into "legitimate" marriage. He sought out women who had divorced and remarried according to tribal custom and explained to them that not only had they no claim on their ex-husbands' property in either divorce or widowhood (see chapter 3) but the children of "illegal cohabitation" were also without legal rights to property, for "illegitimate children do not . . . inherit from their father."[25]

Technically, however, Leonard's threats did not reflect OIA inheritance policies. In a very complicated heirship case where a deceased boy's parents were not married and he had been raised by his maternal aunt, Leonard told the CIA that children of such unions still "seem[ed] more like illegitimate children than anything else." The child's paternal family shared in the inheritance with his maternal aunt, whom Leonard claimed was the only "true" heir. For purposes of inheritance, the OIA recognized as legitimate the children of couples "cohabited together according to the custom and manner of Indian life." For all other purposes, the Office deemed these children "otherwise illegitimate."[26]

Leonard's threat to disinherit "illegitimate" children was hollow, but Agent Charles Werner's threat to refuse them enrollment on the tribal rolls was not. Werner (agent from 1907 to 1912) was perhaps the best example of an official zealous about moral matters. In 1911 he searched out cohabiting couples and "In some cases, the children of an illegal marriage were not recognized or placed on the rolls until the parents were married legally." Werner witnessed sixteen marriages at the agency during his tenure, but the licenses do not record whether these couples had previously lived together in tribal marriages. The following year Werner arrested two couples for fornication and two for unlawful cohabitation; agency accounts do not mention what happened to those charged.[27]

In his campaign to "improve" Ute morals, Werner intruded into men's and women's personal lives. He claimed, in 1911, that he kept Ute girls in school until he could find suitable husbands for them: "They are encouraged to marry ex-students. This precaution is necessary to build up the morals of the tribe and to build a better future generation."[28] Werner's remarks are impossible to substantiate. Did he really find suitable husbands for women he kept in school? While it is doubtful that Werner forced couples into arranged marriages, he did, in three cases, set himself up as the arbitrator of what constituted a "proper" family.

In 1910 Werner wrote to Harry Hummer, superintendent of the Canton Indian Insane Asylum in South Dakota, asking to place the Brown sisters. He described both of them as insane (although it is more likely that they were mentally retarded) and judged their sexual conduct improper enough to warrant their removal from the reservation. Jane Brown was an unwed mother with two sons: Harry, aged eight, and Ernest, aged five. Susan Brown was "the wife of James A. — a well meaning Ute." The couple had two children but one died in infancy due to a congenital defect, leaving Mary, aged seven months. Werner concluded Susan was unable to care for Mary and persuaded the couple to give her up for adoption to a Hispanic family. He wrote, "I did not realize the consequences of letting these two women remain at large until those children were born."[29]

Canton could not immediately take the Brown women; neither could the Colorado state asylum. Werner wrote to the commissioner in 1912 again pleading with him to get Susan into Canton. "She is about to become a mother for the third time," he lamented, "and it is deplorable that such conditions should exist." The commissioner responded that a Canton patient had just died and that Susan could probably now be placed. She was approximately four months pregnant when she and her sister Jane finally arrived in South Dakota in October of 1912.[30]

Dr. Hummer diagnosed Jane as suffering from "idiocy" and Susan's condition as "imbecility, congenital." His prognosis for both was "unfavorable" for their physical condition was "poor." In March, Susan gave birth to a baby girl. Revising his earlier estimate of her pregnancy, Hummer wrote that Susan's girl was premature and "its chances for surviving do not appear very bright just now. The mother is doing quite well at this time."[31]

The baby survived, and, in May of 1913, the asylum superintendent requested that she be returned to the reservation. "While I realize the burden that the child is at the insane asylum," replied Agent Stephen Abbott (Werner's successor), "it would be almost the same as murder to let the helpless father have the child." He suggested she be sent to a charitable institution. In June of 1913, however, field matron Cora Hutchinson took the baby from the asylum to Susan's father, Steven Brown. Hutchinson reported that Susan was near death, and Abbot requested that the asylum return her body should she die. Susan did die shortly thereafter, and Hummer allowed her remains to be sent to her family.[32]

After Susan's death, Steven Brown requested that his daughter Jane also be returned to him, but the OIA refused his wish on the recommendation of Dr. Hummer. The doctor described Jane as "an idiot, who fails to comprehend anything said to her and is unable to talk. She has no intelligence whatsoever." He claimed it would be inhumane to release her. In 1916 Jane died of tuberculosis while still at the asylum. Her body was "given a Christian burial in the Asylum cemetery."[33]

Commenting on the case several years later, Agent Walter Runke noted that Susan had no right to enter into a marriage, for she was "always of unsound mind and idiotic from young on," yet Susan's husband James appeared to cherish and care for his wife; he did not want her removed to the asylum. Additionally, Jane's parents did not consider her or her children a burden but, rather, made clear their desire to keep the extended family together. As far as the records indicate, these women were removed from their homes because an OIA agent — Werner — was horrified by their having children and estimated they could not be effective mothers. That the women's families wanted them meant little to Werner. James A., he wrote, "tries to care for [Susan] but is absolutely unable to do so." Apparently viewing himself as the proper authority on what constituted an acceptable family, Werner broke up both the Allens' and the Browns' households.[34]

Werner also interfered in K. M.'s marriage, because he did not approve of either her spouse or her extramarital sexual conduct. K. M., the daughter of a Uintah-Ouray woman and a Southern Ute man, married Southern Ute Jim P., who was deaf. Werner estimated that she was only about fifteen years old at the time. According to Werner, he tried to prevent the marriage, most probably because of the husband's deafness. Despite his efforts, the couple sneaked off to the Catholic church and took their vows. On her wedding night, K. M. abandoned her husband and went drinking with various men, staying with different ones over the next few weeks. Werner arrested her for "carousing," and placed her in the custody of field matron Mellie Martin until he could send her to Uintah-Ouray. K. M. escaped the matron and made the rounds of her boyfriends' abodes.[35]

Werner recaptured K. M. and, again, held her "in custody." He apparently annulled her marriage and tried to send her to the Haskell Institute. Her father refused to allow this and, unlike the case of the Brown women (perhaps because she was considered mentally competent), Werner could not send her. Then for unknown reasons, K. M. suddenly settled down. She lived with her father at Southern Ute until 1912 when she remarried and began farming. She had her funds transferred from Uintah-Ouray (where her mother lived), bought horses and wagons, leased an allotment she inherited from her brother at Uintah-Ouray, and made a nice profit.[36] This time no agent interfered in her marriage.

Werner's primary consideration in both these cases may have been that one of the partners was handicapped, but in both instances the woman's sexual behavior precipitated the intervention, and his solution in both situations was to remove, or try to remove, the "offensive" woman. The agent's power over the Utes' lives permitted him to judge the validity of their most intimate decisions and to veto their choices. Thus, women endured serious infringements on their personal autonomy from agents; some Ute women faced similar attempts at control from Ute men.

Before confinement to the reservation, Ute men had no formal means by which to prevent their wives from leaving them. Indeed, Ute custom scorned men who attempted to fetch home "runaway" wives. Soon after resettlement, however, Ute men learned to call on agents for help in returning their spouses. Agent David Day described one such incident in 1890. In this instance, a wife had left her husband for another man, and both of the extended families — who "were of more than ordinary repute" — got involved in the dispute. Day suggested they settle the matter in tribal court, but at the proceedings the couple's "respective advocates began arming at a rate necessitating a prompt dissolution of the court." Agent Day then "adjusted" the matter, "Much to the satisfaction of himself and the disgust of the Indians who cannot understand why an elopement on the part of a female is not treated as a capital offense, with the husband as chief executioner."[37] Day did not allow violent punishment of the woman and implies in the record that she did not return to her husband.

In a similar situation in 1910, a Southern Ute man, Benjamin N., "lost" his wife, E. N., to "Locoe Jim," a Navajo Springs Ute. Navajo Springs agent U. L. Gready wrote to Werner at Southern Ute, noting, "If the culprits reach your agency, please have them locked up and put to hard labor until such time as I can send for them." Whether or not Werner acted on this request, E. N. appeared on the 1912 census with Benjamin.[38] Given Werner's propensity to meddle, he was probably responsible for reuniting Benjamin and E. N.

In 1924 Jon T., a non-Ute man who had married a Ute woman, persuaded Edward McKean to write to Superintendent C. J. Crandall of the Northern Pueblo agency in Santa Fe, requesting that he return to Jon T. his wife, K. T., mother of E. T., who had left her husband, children, and grandchildren to live "in a state of adultery" with Joe V. at one of the Northern Pueblos. K. T., who was "about forty-one," left Jon T., "an old man," for Joe V., "a young man about twenty-six years of age." She told McKean that she had divorced Jon "according to the custom of Indian people" and remarried Joe V. in a ceremony in Redmesa, Colorado. She brought her work team and wagon to the pueblo and set up a farm with her second husband. McKean bemoaned the fact that the case had dragged on for three years and was "the source of considerable trouble to me inasmuch as I have been unable to make a satisfactory adjustment."[39]

Puzzled as to the legality of the situation, since the OIA had recognized Indian marriage and divorce in probate cases, McKean wrote to Assistant Commissioner E. B. Meritt. Adding yet another legal stipulation to the convoluted question of Indian marriage, Meritt replied that K. T. could not marry by Indian custom because she had never lived on her allotment; rather, she had sold it and lived on Jon T.'s land under the jurisdiction of the state of Colorado; her "legal marriage to a citizen of the United States made her a citizen and subject to the laws of the State." Since K. T. was not legally divorced, she was living in adultery, and Meritt noted she should comply with the state law "before any more drastic steps are taken." Whether or not the OIA intended to prosecute the Pueblo man for marrying an already married woman is not mentioned.[40]

K. T.'s second marriage was dissolved within six years, for she appears on the 1930 census living with her 21-year-old son John and his three-year-old son Henry. Obviously, then, she was not forcibly brought back to Jon despite McKean's repeated orders. Given the family history, McKean's failure to return her to the reservation is not surprising. Apparently the couple had been separated before, for they were living apart when E. T. ran away from the Allen day school in 1913 and at the time of her expulsion from the Santa Fe school in 1915. Jon's remarks in 1915 implied that he cared little about K. T.'s activities. Later, however, he apparently cared greatly that she was living with a 26-year-old man.[41]

Jon T.'s sudden demand that his wife be returned represented a double standard, for he had himself been sexually active with numerous women. An oral history of one of his descendants claimed that he had "several" Hispanic wives before he married K. T. and that he might have had lovers after the marriage. His obituary in the reservation newspaper *Ignacio Chief-*

tain reported that he had at one time had five Apache wives.[42] McKean may have been aware of Jon's repute, but it did not deter him from demanding that K. T. come back to the reservation. Despite both men's efforts, K. T. returned in her own time and refused to move back in with Jon.

On one occasion, a Ute man asked Agent William D. Leonard to "restore to him his wife" from Navajo Springs. According to John B., his brother-in-law Cha-cow abducted his eighteen-year-old wife T. B. shortly after their wedding in 1906. It appears that his request was unsuccessful, however, for Bird is listed alone on the 1912 census and is missing from the 1923 census. His wife does not appear in the death records before 1912, so perhaps she stayed with her brother.[43] Perhaps she was never "abducted" at all but rather left her husband voluntarily.

In 1930 a Ute man appealed to the CIA — "the Big Man to look all over the Indians" — to get his wife back. Roy W. wrote: "I wanted you to help me about my wife, the other boy take my wife away from me . . . but the Edward peacore *[sic]* don't try to help me, we are married by the law in Durango[,] Colo." Agent Peacore answered that he had indeed returned L. W. to her husband once already, and she had promised "that she would never do this again if Roy would take her back." Roy gambled away their money, however, and refused to support either her or their baby, and she left again. Peacore described Roy W. as "one of the most worthless young Utes that we have at Ignacio" and noted that his wife would divorce him as soon as she had the funds. Apparently, agents defended runaway wives if their husbands did not support them.[44]

In instances where Ute men solicited the agents' assistance to control or return their wives, considerations of gender seem to have united agents and Ute husbands against Ute women, yet this collaboration must be viewed carefully. Some Ute husbands, coming from a tradition in which they had virtually no control over their wives, were quick to take advantage of a newly imposed system of social control. They left no statements explaining why they wanted their wives returned and therefore their motives are impossible to judge. Agents, on the other hand, always explained their actions in terms of carrying out policy to maintain family stability; nowhere did they call for male control over women. Further, the official OIA code called for sanctions against husbands and fathers who deserted or failed to support their families. There were no marital regulations aimed specifically at women; thus, control of women was never official policy.[45]

Nevertheless, there is no evidence that Agent Peacore penalized Roy W. (or any other man) for gambling away his family's funds, and there are no recorded cases of agents punishing Ute husbands for infidelity or desertion, even though these problems existed. In 1917, when John Tyler refused to support his wife Topsy Plato, Walter West did not enforce the OIA code. Interpreting the agents' refusal to enforce the OIA regulations punishing men is problematic. Perhaps they felt that restraining women's sexual behavior was a better strategy for preserving the moral and social design of the reservation. As OIA rhetoric emphasized women as the moral foundation of the "civilization" program, Ute women's sexual agency may have seemed a greater threat to the moral order the Office was trying to impose. Agents may have had personal motives for punishing women rather than men. Perhaps these individuals hated sexually independent women because they did not conform to the agents' own private ideals of proper feminine behavior. Finally, agents may have whipped Indian women because they viewed them as children who needed corporal punishment for "bad" behavior. Whatever their reasoning, Southern Ute agents carried out a sexual politics that punished women and not men, even though their official *Rulebook* called for the reverse.[46] For all their efforts to regulate sex and marriage, what effect did these men have on marital stability?

Marriage at Southern Ute

What did marriage patterns look like at Southern Ute during this period? Evaluation is difficult because of conflicting evidence. Agents' reports in 1893, 1894, 1906, and 1907 note the brittleness of marital ties among the Utes and a lack of cooperation in complying with state marriage laws. Around 1910 agents began asserting that "most Utes" married according to law, although "a few" tribal marriages still slipped by them. Agency records confirm a growing number of legal unions on the reservation over the first two and a half decades of the twentieth century. From 1901 to 1911, Ute couples filed thirty-two marriage licenses, but two of them were not completed (tribal marriages were not recorded); from 1912 to 1925 fifty-one couples were legally wed and twenty-one were tribally wed.[47] Thus, while tribal marriages continued, increasing numbers of couples were applying for marriage licenses.

Why did Utes take out marriage licenses? Again, evidence is fragmentary. Surviving copies of the thirty-four certificates from 1901 to 1911, however, suggest some hypotheses. Since twenty-seven legal marriages occurred under Leonard and Werner, it is likely that the agents pressured these couples — especially since one of the two agents presided over thirteen of the ceremonies. Religious convictions may have motivated some couples to apply for licenses, for twelve Catholic and five Protestant weddings occurred. The actual marriage decrees for the period 1912–25 did not survive; the only evidence available for this time are numbers in statistical reports and scattered remarks by the agents. Again, religion may have played a role in the decision to wed legally. For the years 1912–25, 140 to 315 Utes claimed to be Catholic while thirty to fifty affiliated with Presbyterianism. Increased enrollments in OIA schools during this period may also have affected the number of state-sanctioned marriages. Agent Edward McKean, in 1918, credited schooling: "the younger women who have been married during the past year all insist upon legal church marriages."[48] Whatever the impetus, the Utes increasingly accommodated OIA demands in this area during the early years of the twentieth century.

What do these figures reveal about actual marriage practices? How many couples in these lawful marriages broke up and remarried without the agent's knowledge? Agents' reports cannot answer these questions. Other data, however, offer some sense of how stable these unions were over time. In 1931 Inspector G. E. E. Lindquist wrote, "A number of the Indians are married legally while others still practice Indian custom marriages. I can not see any difference: when they get mad at each other they leave their camp[s] and go to another one." Marvin Opler, an anthropologist who lived at Southern Ute in the early 1930s, mentioned that the majority of Utes preferred serial monogamy to lifelong coupling with one partner. Opler was referring to conditions during his fieldwork and in the aboriginal community. Anthropologist Omer C. Stewart, who also resided on the reservation in the 1930s, made the same observation. The Utes' custom of easy divorce would certainly accommodate serial monogamy.[49] While the Utes took out more marriage licenses, holding said licenses may not have had much of an effect on actual behavior.

But what was normative behavior? Did the majority of Ute couples practice serial monogamy or did observers generalize from a small sample to Ute culture in general? Is there any way of knowing how many couples remained together until parted by death? The original allottees constitute a traceable group (to some extent) in the records. Sixty-one couples received allotments together in 1895. Fifty-five of these men and women appeared on the agency death ledgers from 1896 to 1923. These records noted that nine couples were divorced and forty-six were widowed. It is possible, then, that most couples at the time of allotment had fairly stable marriages. An agent who worked with this group in 1890, Charles Bartholomew, wrote, "Dissolution of marriages appears to be upon the desire of one or both parties, but such dissolution is of infrequent occurrence."[50] On the other hand, perhaps the death records are misleading for they do not indicate whether the couple was actually living together at the time of the given spouse's death — they only record "official divorces." There may have been more tribal-custom divorces than appear in the death records; agents' reports from 1893 and 1894 commenting on shifting marital ties may have been a more accurate description of normative behavior.

It may be impossible to determine normative marital behavior in this period. It is possible, however, to generalize about Ute conceptions of marriage and to ask if the conditions that created these ideals changed drastically after confinement to the reservation. The family was critical to survival in pre-reservation days. The sparse resources of the Great Basin limited hunting and gathering groups to small clusters of siblings and their spouses, usually living — at least in the early years of marriage — near the woman's parents. The conjugal relationship played the pivotal role in these family units, for couples depended on one another for material and social support. If marriage was crucial economically, then why did the Utes permit easy divorce? Why did family members not force couples to stay together? It is possible for a culture to value the institution of marriage while also allowing that any given marriage may be brief. Families could afford to allow divorce because individuals were unlikely to stay single for long. Because of the relative isolation of the band, family members may actually have encouraged incompatible partners to split up to preserve group harmony.[51]

Similar conditions prevailed after relocation. Because the reservation economy was never far above subsistence level, families still needed two or more wage earners. Thus, the economic importance of the family did not change, nor most likely did family pressure to maintain permanent marital ties increase. After the Utes were forced into a sedentary lifestyle, there may have been a larger pool of potential new spouses to choose from and individuals may have remained single for even shorter periods of time. The reservation did not lessen the need for relatively informal divorce; it may, in fact, have increased it.

This is not to say that families did not face new problems on the reservation. One might well ask what part assimilationist demands played in transient marriages. Perhaps the tensions of reservation life — the loss of political autonomy and traditional subsistence activities, the removal of Indian children to boarding schools where they were indoctrinated in Euro-American culture, and the systematic persecution of Native American religion — caused some Indian marriages to unravel. One way to gauge the negative effects of reservation life on Indian marriages is to look for evidence of domestic violence.[52]

According to agency accounts, domestic violence appears to have been rare during the entire period of OIA "civilization." In 1882 and 1884 the agency physician noted lethal violence against women by their husbands. In July of 1882 a man killed his wife "for non-conformance to the marriage rite." The doctor did not explain the nature of this offense, but the woman may have been killed for adultery. Agent Warren Patten investigated the killing, along with three other murders of men, and concluded that the homicides were "justifiable in every case and no attempt has been made to punish the parties that did the killing." In April of 1884 Patten casually noted in a letter to the CIA, "A buck killed his squaw, [he] shot her in the head." Patten did not even mention this occurrence in his annual report of that year.[53] These are the only two accounts of husbands harming their wives. Even in all of the correspondence of "law and order" and all of the documents concerning the liquor traffic, there are no other recorded incidents of interpersonal violence between husbands and wives. This does not necessarily mean that domestic violence did not occur; it may mean that incidents went unreported or that the offending parties were not charged. It could indicate that agents thought, as Warren Patten did, that the murder of a "squaw" by her "buck" simply did not merit comment. It could also mean, however, that domestic violence was rare on the Ute reservation during this period.

Serial monogamy rather than domestic violence may have been the primary response to reservation stress. One or the other partner may simply have left the marriage when tension levels rose. Marital discord may, then, have led to separation rather than to domestic violence. Without specific evidence from Ute sources, it is impossible to say for certain; still, it is reasonable to assume that the strain of reservation life may have contributed to the brevity of some marriages.

Sexual Harassment and Assault

While spousal abuse seems to have been uncommon, some Ute women did suffer from sexual violence during this period. In 1878 two "white stockmen" camped on the reservation attempted sexual contact with two Ute "squaws." The women fled and the men shot at them. Agent Henry Page reported that some Ute men, presumably the women's family, confronted the whites "who claimed it was all a joke, which explanation they accepted." Why the men were willing to accept this kind of behavior as a joke is unknown. Page included a description of this affair in a special report "Indian Troubles on the Reservation." Confrontations between Indians and trespassers on the reservation often resulted when Ute men sought to protect Ute women from intruders.[54]

An incident involving Chipeta, Chief Ouray's widow, highlights the vulnerability of Ute women to harassment by Anglo men. In 1887 Chipeta and her friends were gathering food with their children, "there being no bucks in the camp." A party of armed white men came into camp and began claiming each of the women as their "squaws," describing "in lewd manner" what they would do to them. Chipeta was terrified but, fortunately, the men left without molesting the women. When Chipeta and her party attempted to leave, however, the men reappeared and pursued them. She lost the men at a ledge of rocks, and then watched them return to her camp "and burn the tepees and the entire camp outfit." The women managed to make their way to safety.[55] Whites engaged in this assault as part of a larger campaign of harassment designed to discourage Utes from hunting and gathering off the reservation, but women had their own unique experience of terror when the armed men threatened to rape them in front of their children.

In the few instances of alleged rape on the reservation, agents did not take the women's complaints very seriously. In 1909 Charles Werner described his investigation of the rape of a sixteen-year-old girl, "slightly deranged in mind," by two eighteen-year-old Ute men named Ben R. and Peter J. The young woman, I. E., was limping, and she told her stepmother she had broken her leg trying to resist the two men's attack. The agency physician, Dr. Robbins, examined her, "found no signs of abuse or being mistreated," and concluded that her joints were probably tubercular. He prescribed some medicine for her.[56]

The "boys" claimed I. E. had consented to have sex with them, and Werner fined them "by putting them at hard labor," after which Peter J. was to leave the reservation. "However," Werner wrote, "this did not suit John Taylor, a negro squaw man. He filed a complaint of rape against Ben R. and Peter J." Since I. E. was not a member of John's family, the reason for his interest in this case is unclear. As I. E.'s leg was not healing, Dr. Robbins brought in a second physician, who detected a fracture in her femur and concluded that I. E. might have suffered "a small amount of violence." Werner claimed the fracture probably resulted from her tripping, since "she had walked about for six weeks after the rape was supposed to have been committed." He also defended Dr. Robbins' treatment of I. E. despite his failure to diagnose the fractured leg.[57]

A jury in La Plata County found Ben R. guilty of rape. Most of I. E.'s family and Agent Werner were among the twelve witnesses for the prosecution. The presiding judge, Charles Pike, refused to sentence Ben R., claiming that since the action took place on I. E.'s allotment, he had no jurisdiction. Ben R. went home to farm his allotment, showing up in a picture of "progressive Indians" in the 1920 annual report to the CIA.[58]

The laws governing crimes on Indian land were somewhat tangled at the time of Ben R.'s trial. According to the Major Crimes Act of 1885, federal courts had jurisdiction over eight offenses: "murder, manslaughter, rape, assault with intent to kill, assault with a dangerous weapon, arson, burglary, and larceny." At the time of the rape, however, there were questions concerning federal Indian law. The granting of patents had diminished federal control by extending state and territorial law over allotted Indians. As Indians met with injustice in local judicial systems, however, some OIA officials called for the federal government to reassert its authority in legal matters.[59]

In 1909 a Supreme Court decision — *U.S. v. Celestine* — upheld federal jurisdiction in rape cases and U.S. statute law declared "all Indians" anywhere committing the eight crimes against anyone were to be "tried therefor *[sic]* in the same courts and in the same manner and shall be subject to the same penalties as are all other persons charged with the commission of said crimes."[60] It appears that Ben R. should have been tried in the federal rather than the county courts, but this law may not have been in effect when Pike heard the case. While Pike may have been legitimately concerned with jurisdictional questions, the result was that the officials of the United States government, both in the courts and on the reservation, failed to administer justice in I. E.'s case.[61]

A similar situation occurred in 1929 when Antonio Buck, a distinguished tribal leader, wrote to the commissioner describing how he saw several "Mexicans" take unfair sexual advantage of two Ute women incapacitated by liquor:

> May you like what I said in this my letter or not but I don't like that I am reporting this to you. . . . [The Mexicans] take these Ute girls behind store building where no one can't see. So the two Mexicans give the two Ute girls drink of whiskey. Then these girls get drunk these fellows fuck the girls. The Ute girls was pretty drunk, don't know

anything atall[. They were] just laying down, can't get up. Then those two Mexican call the rest of the Mexican boys. They fuck those girls while they drunk.

Buck clearly interpreted the men's behavior as sexual assault and he pleaded with the Office to "chase [these men] out of the town and stop the trouble here at Ignacio, [Colorado]." Commissioner Charles Burke replied to Buck instructing him to work with Superintendent Edward J. Peacore to solve the problem. He also sent Peacore a copy of Buck's letter, telling him to "render such assistance to the authorities as may be practicable in prosecuting the guilty parties."[62]

Replying to Buck's charges, Peacore wrote: "concerning outrages committed by two Mexicans against two Ute women. I am sorry Mr. Buck misrepresented this to the Office." Peacore claimed he "was notified that these two Mexicans had two Ute women [at the] back of the pool hall in Ignacio" and he investigated "immediately." The women were indeed very inebriated, he noted, and he had them sent home. He then arrested the two "Mexicans"—Joe M. and Manuel A.—on charges of bootlegging. Peacore's letter stressed his efforts to purge Ignacio of liquor; Buck's concerns were dismissed. The case was tried by a prohibition officer, again with no word of the women; the men were acquitted of bootlegging for lack of evidence.[63] Despite Antonio Buck's eyewitness account, Peacore did not investigate what happened to the two women nor did he file assault charges against Joe M. and Manuel A.

Shortly after the incident in Ignacio, Ute Indian Charles A. killed Joe M. One day Charles A. followed his wife V. A. and her two children to Joe M.'s house in Ignacio. Charles A. claimed that he saw "A bed made up on the floor and Joe M. was on top of [his] wife in this bed with a blanket over them" and the baby lying near them. According to Charles, when his wife spotted him in the window, she grabbed the baby and fled. He charged into the house, confronting Joe M., who was trying to pull up his pants. Joe M. shouted "What do you want here you Son-of-a-Bitch[?]" and Charles A., fearing Joe M. was "trying to get his knife," stabbed him in the chest and left. Charles A. then rode back to the agency and told a Ute man, John Burch, what he had done. Burch turned Charles A. over to Peacore, and Charles confessed to murder. H. J. Stricken of the OIA investigated the case.[64]

During the inquiry, Peacore told Stricken about Joe M.'s arrest for liquor violations; again, he did not mention the alleged molestation of the Ute women. The Ignacio sheriff, Ed Painter, disclosed that Joe M. had earlier "committed the offense of giving two Indian women whiskey and getting them intoxicated," but he did not recount Antonio Buck's allegations either. The OIA did not comment on Peacore's handling of either the earlier incident or the murder of Joe M.[65]

Some observers of Peacore's administration, however, left voluminous comments on his moral leadership. In 1931 Mrs. Charles Wiegel, chairman of the Indian Welfare Division of the CFWC and member of the Colorado State Commission on Indians, informed CIA Rhodes that her organizations considered the OIA to be a "direct guardian" of Indian girls on the reservation. Wiegel alluded to certain "reports of mis-conduct and mal-administration" concerning the treatment of young women on the reservation and urged a full inspection by the "proper authorities."[66]

The investigation highlighted Peacore's ambiguous moral leadership. Various employees accused Peacore of having an affair with Miss Rosemary T., a Home Economics teacher at the Ute Mountain boarding school. Mrs. Hattie Haren, school cook, claimed that Peacore threatened both her job and her husband Mack's position as school engineer "if she did not have guilty intercourse with him." His behavior, they argued, set a low moral tone for the reservation. But Wiegel's specific allegations were of exploitation of young Indian women at the school.[67]

Wiegel collected affidavits for OIA investigators Roy Nash and H. J. Hagerman. The former school matron at the Ute Mountain boarding school, Lottie McCall, and Mr. Hashbarger, former principal, testified. McCall claimed that Peacore hired her husband as a night watchman for the girls' dormitory at Ute Mountain because "it was a 'regular whore-house.'" According to McCall, when he was fired without cause "the immoral conduct among the boys and girls" began again. The worst offender at the dorm was Eric R., nephew of the agency trader, who was staying with his uncle. Eric bragged to McCall that he slept with R. C. on numerous occasions. R. C. had agreed to have sex with Eric, but McCall still blamed Peacore for not taking steps to remove him and protect the young girl's morals.[68]

Unlike his predecessors, Peacore did not beat or expel anyone, even after R. C. gave birth to a child she claimed was Eric's. Instead, he asked Eric to marry R. C. When he refused, Peacore ordered his uncle to send him back to his parents. R. C. married (by custom) Henry C., a Ute Indian, and declared him the father of her child. The Utes seemed satisfied with this state of affairs and Peacore dismissed the issue. Peacore may have handled this matter in such a relaxed way because he was Native American. As a member of the Chipewa tribe, Peacore may have been more willing to let the Utes adjust such matters themselves. An unnamed OIA official, however, did not appreciate his casual attitude. He wrote: "Peacore could have done more than this, it seems to me. Marrying the girl is not an answer and sending the man away with nothing settled is no solution."[69]

Peacore provided "no solution" for S. D. H. either. During the investigation of reservation morals, S. D. H. swore an affidavit that Edward T. had forced her into Eric R.'s car and "took me down to the bridge and raped me." After the alleged assault, Edward T., Eric R., and R. C. went to Cortez where Edward T. "bought [them] some candy." S. D. H. asked to leave when they returned to R. C.'s camp, but Edward T. took her to his house. "I slept with Ed Saturday night and Sunday night," she recounted, "I told him I want to go home but he say, 'no I don't want you to go.' He locked me in when he play[ed] ball Sunday afternoon. This is true, I told it to Mrs. McCall."[70]

Since Edward T. was married and his wife was pregnant, Lottie McCall and her husband had tried to discourage his interest in S. D. H. McCall claimed she asked Peacore for help in this regard but he refused. One day McCall and Principal Hashbarger discovered S. D. H. at Edward T.'s house "bloody from her head to her heels." They took her to McCall's home where she "slept for a day and a half without waking." After a few days, S. D. H. returned home and Edward T. continued his relationship with her. According to McCall, her morals further deteriorated: "The girl is now living with first one man and then another," she testified.[71]

McCall demanded that Peacore punish Edward T., but he replied that he could do nothing unless the accused had "been caught in the act." Still, Peacore dismissed Edward from his job as agency interpreter and fined him thirty days' pay. Peacore then gave the money to Edward T.'s wife. He forgot the incident until Mrs. Wiegel opened the investigation and read S. D. H.'s statement to a gathering of Ignacio residents who disapproved of Peacore. Peacore then questioned S. D. H. himself. She described being raped at the bridge but also said that the sex at Edward T.'s house was consensual. Peacore decided that her bloody condition when McCall found her had been due to her "monthly period of sickness" and not to abuse.[72]

Peacore produced no counteraffidavit in which S. D. H. retracted her claim of rape at the bridge; her only statement on record states that she was assaulted. In all the pages of testimony in the investigation of Peacore, only three are devoted to S. D. H.'s story. There was no follow-up to decide if she had indeed been brutalized. The sole purpose of mentioning the occurrence was to decide whether or not Peacore was competent; justice for

S. D. H. was not an issue. Allison Kroeger's investigation on behalf of the Colorado Indian Commission did not even mention S. D. H. Even Wiegel did not press for an inquiry.[73]

Why did such a serious accusation go unexplored? Did Peacore's testimony damage S. D. H.'s credibility? Did her continuing to see Edward make her seem less like a victim of rape? Did she request that the issue be dropped because it was painful? Any of these points may have derailed an investigation, but S. D. H.'s complaint was most likely buried beneath the personal and political squabbling that marked the Peacore administration. Complaints of Peacore's activities on and off the reservation were voluminous. His staff was severely factionalized, and acrimonious feelings ran deep — especially for the McCalls, who lost their jobs, and the Harens, who claimed Peacore sexually harassed Mrs. Haren.

Moreover, both Nash and Kroeger were horrified that Wiegel would make public accusations of a sexual nature, especially regarding the alleged affair between Rosemary T. and Peacore. "We have many young girls employed at these schools whose reputations can be jeopardized," Nash wrote, "my personal opinion is that a very substantial damages suit should be brought on behalf of Miss T. against Nellie M. Wiegel." Of Wiegel's exposure of R. C.'s alleged affair, Nash declared "Indian girls have reputations to lose as well as white," but he did not suggest a lawsuit, nor did he appeal to the commissioner as a father or ask him to put himself in the position of the slandered girl's mother, as he had done with Rosemary's case. He never expressed any concern for S. D. H.'s good name.[74] The investigation, then, was concerned with sexual proprieties of white women and the competency of Peacore.

For all their paternalism and expressions of concern for "morality" on the reservation, most agents did not seriously investigate reports of rape. True, Agent Werner sentenced Ben R. and Peter J. to hard labor and removed Peter J. from the reservation for assaulting I. E., and Peacore fined Edward T. thirty days' pay for sexual contact with R. C. Nevertheless, these agents never filed formal rape charges. Even when Wiegel and McCall documented R. C.'s and S. D. H.'s grievances no one sought legal redress. A Ute man, Antonio Buck, and an African-American man who married into the tribe, John Taylor, were the only people to call for legal recourse for Ute women in cases of alleged rape. It appears that Southern Ute agents viewed sexual assault as a breach of reservation regulations rather than as a serious violent crime.

Conveniently for the OIA, most of the men accused of molesting or seducing Ute women were outside the Ute reservation power structure. In only one instance was a superintendent accused of sexual contact with an Indian woman. In this case, the scene was the Jicarilla agency, a subagency of Southern Ute in the late nineteenth century. In 1891 the OIA investigated Mr. Bishop, the agency's superintendent, for allegedly seducing an Apache woman who then bore his son. Bishop was cleared of the charges. Agent Charles Bartholomew, expressing his satisfaction with the verdict, wrote, "not believing that a single employee at either agency would stoop to such a degraded act," he had always known Bishop would be exonerated.[75]

Bartholomew conceded that, since the woman in question was a graduate of an OIA school whose "social and domestic habits" were above those of her unschooled sisters, she might have been somewhat attractive. Still, upon contact with her tribe, the woman rapidly deteriorated "to the old rut," and Bartholomew exhorted the commissioner never to return a woman to her tribe for she would, "by her improved appearance temporarily dazzle the eyes of her dusky suitor" and then find, after marriage, that she could not "in any degree elevate her dusky husband to her own level." The implication of Bartholomew's remarks was that this woman briefly sought out Bishop because, before she "backslid," she had "advanced" far beyond the available beaux.[76]

According to Bartholomew, only under extraordinary circumstances would a respectable Anglo agent or full-time employee find a Ute woman an acceptable sexual partner. No other agent left any remarks concerning the sexual attractiveness of Ute women, but there is no evidence of sexual liaisons between Anglo agents and Ute women. Mr. Hashbarger, principal of the Ute Mountain boarding school, had an Indian wife when he came to the reservation but otherwise there were no marriages between Anglos and Indians at Southern Ute. Ironically, the only Native American who served as superintendent during this time, Edward Peacore, ran off with an Irish employee.[77] According to available evidence, then, OIA agents did not hold Ute women as concubines.

Conclusions

Despite the rhetoric of moral "regeneration of the race through the women," enforcement of OIA policies on sexual conduct at Southern Ute disclosed contradictions in Euro-Americans' attitudes toward Indian women's sexuality. From the earliest days of colonization Euro-Americans regarded Native American women in terms of a "Princess-Squaw" dichotomy. OIA policy preaching the importance of Indian women to tribal moral "improvement" is a variant of the "Princess" view. As Pocahontas "rescued" John Smith by abandoning her culture, so Indian women on reservations could "rescue" their people from savagery by abandoning their traditions of sexual independence. That OIA personnel also made women's sexual behavior the focus of castigation and coercion suggests the "Squaw" image, in which Indian women were seen as lustful and sexually aggressive. To impose successfully the Euro-American sexual code on Native Americans, it was necessary to chasten lascivious Indian women. Indian women, then, were symbols of unrestrained sexuality that threatened the moral order of the reservation. In this regard, the experiences of Indian women parallel those of other women of color whose sexuality was stereotyped as morally deficient by the dominant culture.[78]

Agents' attempts to control Ute sexual behavior involved some of the harshest sanctions meted out on the reservation. The whippings of E. T., F. S., and A. B. are the only recorded cases of OIA personnel inflicting corporal punishment on any Utes. Exiling Susan and Jane Brown to an insane asylum because they continued to have children (even though the women's families were willing to care for them) was also a severe action, albeit one common for the times with regard to the mentally handicapped. Arresting and confining K. M., annulling her marriage, and attempting to remove her from the reservation were also drastic measures. Demanding that women caught in premarital sex marry their lovers or that "runaway" wives return to their husbands deeply intruded into the most personal of behavior. Finally, threatening a woman's children with loss of property or funds in order to compel legal marriages represented a very calculated attempt to use women's fears and concerns to manipulate their actions. Whether the agents who employed such tactics had intense feelings about individual "immoral" women or they believed they must change Ute sexual conduct for the benefit of the tribe, they were often harsh.

Unfortunately for Ute women, agents did not always have the same zeal for punishing male offenders. In only one case — that of F. S.'s Hispanic lover — did an agent ever bring legal charges against a man for rape; and in F. S.'s case, she had not (as far as can be discovered) requested that he do so. Accusations of sexual assault were only briefly investigated, the few sentences imposed upon alleged rapists were hardly fitting punishment for a crime of violence, and the one time that a conviction was obtained, jurisdictional problems meant the rapist escaped punishment. The murderers of "squaws" in 1882 and 1884 also went unpunished. These actions implied that few men would suffer for mistreatment of Ute women — and the agent would define what constituted mistreatment regardless of the women's feelings. Finally, the agents did not consistently enforce OIA policy to discipline men who neglected or deserted their families. A sexist "double standard" marked enforcement of sexual policies on the reservation.

While agents' sanctions against women's violations of the reservation moral code were very stern, Ute women's resistance was equally fierce. A. B., E. T., and F. S. all escaped forced marriages, probably due to their choices. If U. W. did not, that was probably also her choice. As far as can be determined, the anonymous woman whom Agent Day judged for desertion along with T. B., K. T., and L. W. all refused to return to their bad marriages, and K. M. withstood "deportation" for her "carousing." If the Brown sisters could not resist expulsion, perhaps it was because their rights were limited by their alleged disabilities. In this most personal realm of decision making, then, this small sampling of Ute women apparently asserted their autonomy — often resisting the combined efforts of both the agent and husbands quick to utilize new means to control their wives.[79]

Were these women's experiences representative of Ute responses to OIA coercion? Given the ambiguous nature of the data, it is nearly impossible to draw definite conclusions about normative sexual conduct. Over time, however, the Utes did take out an increasing number of marriage licenses. Obtaining these documents indicates a willingness to conform to OIA marital customs on some level. On a deeper level, the Utes may not have viewed these certificates as a sign of lifelong commitment; evidence of serial monogamy supports this conclusion. Thus, the resistance to coercion evidenced by this small group of women probably does reflect a larger pattern of response in which Ute men and women maintained some autonomy over their marital practices despite superficial accommodation to assimilationist demands.

Conclusion

For forty-nine years (1895–1934) the OIA attempted to restructure Ute culture according to Euro-American ideas of "civilization." The OIA assaulted traditional Ute culture in every area of life, from subsistence strategy, to political and social structures, to sexual and marital relationships. In each of these spheres, policy makers attempted to transform gender roles. The Office instituted a patriarchal paradigm that was a drastic departure from traditional Ute culture in which women's primary roles as producers, wives, and mothers gave them political, economic, and social equality with men.

In very important ways OIA personnel treated women differently from men. The Office attempted to exclude women from political activities and to limit their economic opportunities on the reservation. Additionally, Ute women suffered special pressures when OIA staff tried to use them as agents of change. This was especially evident in the realm of sexual conduct where agents attempted to use women's concern for their children's security to blackmail them into compliance with Euro-American sexual norms. OIA personnel sometimes exhibited a double standard, such as when they penalized Ute women for "unorthodox" sexual conduct without punishing their partners. Women also experienced their own unique injustice within relations of administrative power when agents refused to take seriously any complaints of rape.

Despite this imposition of patriarchal ideals, women on the Southern Ute reservation were not passive victims — they hardly conformed to the stereotypes imposed on them by the dominant culture. They were not "exceedingly backward and silent and . . . no better off than the most degraded slaves."[1] They spoke up about their concerns and actively challenged the system in several areas. Their actions suggest that, while women were oppressed in the larger context of the reservation, they persisted in positions of influence and equality in the subcontext of continued Ute cultural identity. In this arena Ute women carried out an agenda of selective cooperation and resistance.

Along with male family members, women initially refused sedentism, shifting their residences to other jurisdictions. They joined with their husbands in using Floretta Shields' school as an option to avoid government schools. They were active in protests to get more rations, participated in the debate over removal, and added their voices to investigations of financial issues or criticisms of their agent. In many instances both women and men refused to accept the imposed Euro-American standards concerning sex and marriage; both men and women continued pre-reservation patterns of household residence.

Women also conducted their own campaigns aimed at preserving their autonomy and interests. They sought to protect their rights to annuities during the negotiations over allotments. Daisy Spencer Baker and Mary Baker Pena petitioned the OIA for redress of their personal financial grievances. Women led the resistance to unsafe boarding schools. Several young women wrote to Mrs. Nellie Wiegel of the CFWC to get out of off-reservation schooling. Women were initially very conservative regarding Anglo medical practices, participating in reservation health care only when the OIA provided a female practitioner of healing. In almost all of these efforts, women forced the OIA to modify its plans and accommodate, if only partially, their demands.

A crucial form of resistance to assimilationist policies was the continuation of cultural practices in the areas of extended families and child care, communal work patterns, rituals and ceremonies, and native craft work. Ute women, like other Native American women, contributed heavily to this cause. For women, being caretakers of children also meant being caretakers of Ute traditions; both roles provided self-worth and cultural recognition. Six oral histories of Ute women collected by the Center for Southwest Studies at Fort Lewis College near the reservation indicate that women's roles as producers, teachers, and parents continued to be the basis for full participation in Ute culture throughout the reservation period. In each interview, women spoke of their importance to the family and cultural continuity and stressed that men and women were equally essential to the well-being of the group.[2] Ute culture, then, continued to revere women even when the reservation system did not.

Women were also influential in maintaining family ties with Utes in other jurisdictions, thereby creating a regional community in which Southern Utes could attempt to escape the tensions on their own reservation. Acculturation pressures at Ute Mountain were far fewer than those at Southern Ute because of the lack of allotments. Whether or not Southern Utes found any relief at Uintah-Ouray (where the same assimilationist programs existed) is, of course, questionable. At the very least, shifting residence between reservations acted to frustrate and annoy reservation superintendents, who spent considerable time tracking Southern Utes across other jurisdictions. The option to leave the reservation existed in large part because of the women's actions and was an important component of Ute interference with assimilationist demands.

Resistance to change does not, however, mean that no change occurred. In the material realm, the Utes eventually settled onto their allotments and shifted their subsistence base from hunting and gathering to a mixed economy built on farming, stock raising, wage labor, annuity monies, and, later, oil and gas leases and tourism.[3] Women were part of this transformation. They adopted new technologies and materials for preparing food and clothing, even if they performed these jobs using traditional communal work patterns. They also learned new economic skills such as wage work or buying, selling, and leasing land. Women's economic activities were significant in preventing the Utes from becoming exploited laborers in the regional economy.

Politically, the OIA imposed a tribal council on the Utes; this body proved savvy in the use of lawsuits and petitions to the United States government. Throughout the Dawes era women were involved in council proceedings and in challenging the government, seeking redress of their personal grievances and supporting projects for tribal autonomy. Following the Indian Reorganization Act (which the Utes accepted in 1935), several women served on the tribal council. One woman who served in the 1950s noted that the men on the council seemed to respect and listen to her. All of these councilwomen attended OIA schools and were knowledgeable about the world outside the reservation.[4]

The OIA also altered the institution of marriage. Statistically, the number of legal marriages among the Utes rose in the early part of the twentieth century. Anthropologists who did fieldwork at Southern Ute in the 1930s, however, noted that tribal marriages and serial monogamy continued and that Ute unions were "brittle." Perhaps the only real modification in marriage patterns, then, was in the number of legal documents. The reported transience of Ute marriages may also have reflected the strains that reservation life put on Ute couples.

A few Indian women working with the field matrons adopted what appeared to be Euro-American concepts of feminine gentility, such as wanting music lessons, putting up wallpaper, or making rag rugs and fancy needlework. Since Ute women decorated household objects before residing on the reservation, this behavior did not represent acculturation beyond a shift in artistic mediums. Because none of these items is available for study, it is impossible to know how many of these artistic projects incorporated traditional designs.

The increased number of Utes who attended Euro-American schools undoubtedly encouraged acculturation among the Southern Utes during this period. After initial resistance in the late nineteenth century, the Utes embraced education, sending their children to government schools and, later, to public schools. The report of Inspector G. E. E. Lindquist in 1931 noted that all Ute children had attended school at least until the third or fourth grade.[5] Drawing precise causal lines from education to acculturative transformation is nearly impossible. Nevertheless, many of the changes that occurred following relocation to the reservation must surely be attributed to the influence of Euro-American schooling.

Ute culture changed because of assimilationist programs but the changes were not unilateral, flowing solely from Euro-Americans to Utes. Modifications occurred on the Euro-American side as well. The field matrons who came to Southern Ute to remake women's homes according to middle-class Euro-American standards found their mission frustrated by reservation poverty and disease; health care soon replaced homemaking as their primary focus. Matrons' reports, however, do not indicate that these women were "radicalized" by this experience. None of them addressed the poverty and racism that contributed to the conditions they found. They seemed, instead, to take hope in the few Indian women who joined their cooking and sewing circles. Only one expressed discouragement, and she blamed the "backwardness" of Indian women.

Nellie Wiegel of the CFWC, however, was radicalized. She began as a "do-gooder" with patronizing programs for gardens and baseball, and evolved into an activist for Indian rights. She began as an adjunct to the OIA, and wound up its bitter enemy. Her metamorphosis may have been due, in part, to the fact that she was not employed by the Office. What is especially interesting about her is that she represented a new type of activism among Native Americans and their supporters that was gathering increasing support during the 1920s.[6] The General Federation of Women's Clubs was an important source of support for an Indian policy with a new focus: "regeneration" through tribal economic and political empowerment. Associated with John Collier, founder of the Indian Defense Association and later Indian commissioner under Franklin Roosevelt, this policy shift was later criticized for insensitivity to Native American concerns. In the early twentieth century, however, it seemed a radical solution to the "Indian problem." While Wiegel may have shunned "John Collierism" in her early career, she came to embrace the idea that Indians needed defense rather than "civilization." This was most likely due to her intense personal involvement with individual Utes.[7]

Documenting Ute patterns of cooperation and resistance is fairly easy; accounting for them is more problematic. In the final analysis, it appears that, while the framework of women's lives was radically altered on the reservation, Ute women did not suffer a serious decline in status and power among their people. Numerous scholars have chronicled the oppression of Native American women since contact with Euro-American assimilationist policies.[8] Why, then, were Ute women able to maintain relatively egalitarian gender roles on the reservation?

Ute women's egalitarian position in pre-reservation culture was based on several variables. The struggle for subsistence in an area of limited resources demanded a collectivist ethic that valued women's contributions to group survival — producing food, clothing, and shelter, and bearing children — equally with men's; matrilocality buttressed women's position as producers. The Utes emphasized complementary gender roles. Moreover, their decentralized political system revered age over gender and had no institutions of coercion. Individual autonomy characterized all social relations.

After confinement to the reservation, the Utes underwent the same large-scale changes affecting other Native American peoples: incorporation into the national economy, loss of political autonomy, and the imposition of gendered ideologies that encouraged female subservience. As Daniel Maltz and Joallyn Archambault note in their summary of current literature on gender and power among Native Americans, each of these processes meant that decisions about women's roles were often made by persons and forces outside of a given tribe's control. In some cases, while both men and women lost power and autonomy, women's status and power declined more significantly than men's. Market forces that determined what employment was available to men and women often afforded men greater economic opportunities than women. Political power increasingly came from outside of the group, thus reducing women's traditional power base in kinship systems. In addition, the dominant culture's practice of dealing with men rather than women in economic and political transactions strengthened men's authority in the new political and economic system. Finally, some Native American societies gradually absorbed the idea of a gendered social hierarchy in which women are subservient to men.[9]

For the Southern Utes, however, the reservation context necessitated continued valuation of women's contributions to group survival. The precariousness of the Ute reservation economy mandated that women and men work collectively and value each other's labor. The prevalence of disease on the reservation and the subsequent fluctuations in population meant that bearing and nurturing children were also critical to the Utes' continuation as a people. The Utes thus persisted in esteeming the role of mother, and matrilocality continued to be a popular residence choice. OIA plans that hindered tribal autonomy provided a focal point for cooperation between men and women in resisting outside domination, again stressing the interconnectedness of the sexes and assuring that one would not be valued over the other. While some men sought to use OIA agents to control their wives, there is no evidence that the majority of Ute men sought dominance over Ute women. Had they desired such a goal, they would undoubtedly have been deterred by men and women's interdependence. The gendered society that the OIA hoped to impose, therefore, was thwarted by economic forces. Finally, while the reservation government was centralized, coercive, and deeply sexist, its power was not absolute — Ute women (and men) found ways around government dictates.[10]

Accordingly, relations between Native and Euro-Americans at Southern Ute during the late nineteenth and early twentieth centuries should not be understood by reference to a simple model in which a dominant culture imposed its will on a subordinate one. Rather, a more complex interaction took place, with both sides adapting to one another and altering over time. Women were important agents in this process. Indian women responded to gendered assimilationist policies with shifting patterns of cooperation, resistance, and initiative. Their actions shaped both Ute culture and OIA operations at Southern Ute. The failure and eventual abandonment of the Dawes policies were not simply a matter of deficient strategy on the part of administrators. As actors on the historical scene, Native Americans contributed to the breakdown of OIA policy under the Dawes Act. As active participants in the events at Southern Ute, women played a central role in this development.

Notes

PREFACE

1. "Guidance on Access—RG 75" is available from any branch of the National Archives.

2. In "Teaching American Indian History: A Native American Voice" (*Perspectives* 32, 6 [1994]: 1, 11–16), Donald A. Grinde, Jr. argued for the importance of the native perspective. The essay provoked a caustic reply from James Axtell (*Perspectives* 32, 9 [1992]: 31–33), who felt that Grinde had misrepresented the position of non-native historians. The ultimate outcome of this debate was that both sides appeared sharply polarized with no possibility of compromise. Nothing was resolved, and native and non-native scholars were not given any ideas for fruitful cooperation. Daniel Maltz and Joallyn Archambault ("Gender and Power in Native North America," in *Women and Power in Native North America*, edited by Laura F. Klein and Lillian A. Ackerman [Norman and London: University of Oklahoma Press, 1995], 243–45) also tackle this question and conclude that, while Native American voices are valuable and important to understanding Native American history, "genetics does not enable one to know the past."

INTRODUCTION

1. David A. Day, Southern Ute Agent (SUA), *Annual Report of the Commissioner of Indian Affairs* (Washington, D.C.: Government Printing Office, 1896), 135 (hereafter cited as *ARCIA*).

2. Reservation studies are too numerous to list. Four of the best are as follows: William T. Hagan, *United States–Comanche Relations: The Reservation Years*, new ed. (Norman: University of Oklahoma Press, 1990); Donald J. Berthrong, *The Cheyenne and Arapaho Ordeal: Reservation and Agency Life in the Indian Territory, 1875–1907* (Norman: University of Oklahoma Press, 1976); Richard J. Perry, *Western Apache Heritage: People of the Mountain Corridor* (Austin: University of Texas Press, 1991);

and Morris W. Foster, *Being Comanche: A Social History of an Indian Community* (Tucson: University of Arizona Press, 1991). While all of these works mention native women, they do so only marginally. For an insightful review of the current scholarship on Indian women, see Nancy Shoemaker's introduction to *Negotiators of Change: Historical Perspectives on Native American Women* (New York: Routledge, 1995). Valuable theoretical perspectives on the study of Native American women are also found in *Women and Power in Native North America*, edited by Laura F. Klein and Lillian A. Ackerman (Norman: University of Oklahoma Press, 1995), Gretchen M. Bataille and Kathleen M. Sands, *American Indian Women: Telling Their Lives* (Lincoln: University of Nebraska Press, 1984), and Michael Harkin and Sergei Kan, "Introduction," *Native American Women's Responses to Christianity*, edited by Michael Harkin and Sergei Kan, Special Issue of *Ethnohistory* 42, 3 (1996): 563–69. The most current bibliography is Gretchen M. Bataille and Kathleen M. Sands, *American Indian Women: A Guide to Research* (New York: Garland Publishing, 1991). This guide cites studies of women under directed culture change. Some of the best are as follows: Louise Spindler, "Menomini Women and Culture Change," *American Anthropological Association Memoir No. 91* (N.p.: American Anthropological Association, 1962), 1–113; Mona Etienne and Eleanor Leacock, eds., *Women and Colonization: An Anthropological Perspective* (New York: Praeger Publishing Company Inc., 1979); Patricia Albers and Beatrice Medicine, eds., *The Hidden Half: Plains Indian Women* (Lanham: University Press of America, 1983); Karen Anderson, *Chain Her By One Foot: The Subjugation of Women in Seventeenth-Century New France* (New York: Routledge Press, 1991); and Carol Devens, *Countering Colonization: Native Women and Great Lakes Missions* (Berkeley: University of California Press, 1992). For OIA programs focused on Indian women, see Lisa Emmerich, " 'To Respect and Love and Seek the Ways of White Women': Field Matrons, the Office of Indian Affairs, and Civilization Policy, 1890–1928" (Ph.D. diss., University of Maryland, 1987).

3. Many boxes of field matrons' records were discarded by a National Archives administrator. See Emmerich, " 'Respect and Love.' "

4. Members of the Ute tribal government rejected all of my attempts to involve the tribe in this research project. The woman in charge of tribal education told me that the tribe would write its own history and would not cooperate with any white person's efforts. The few oral histories that have been collected were made available to me through the Center for Southwest Studies at Fort Lewis College in Durango, Colorado, on the condition that I not use the informants' names (hereafter cited as Oral Histories, FLC).

5. I am grateful to my colleague Carolyn Johnston of Eckerd College, St. Petersburg, Florida, for raising the important issue of representativeness. National Association of Indian Affairs, Inc., "Investigation of Southern Ute Jurisdiction, October 1935," Central Classified Files, Consolidated Ute Agency, 806–42821–1936, RG 75, Bureau of Indian Affairs, NARA, Washington, D.C. (hereafter cited as CCF-CU); Omer C. Stewart, "Southern Ute Adjustment to Modern Living," in *Acculturation in the Americas*, edited by Sol Tax (Chicago: University of Chicago Press,

1952), 80–87; Marvin K. Opler, "The Southern Ute of Colorado," in *Acculturation in Seven American Indian Tribes*, edited by Ralph Linton (New York: D. Appleton-Century, 1940), 119–203.

6. The literature on responses of colonized peoples to forced assimilation is voluminous. Some classic theoretical works are as follows: Bronislaw Malinowski, "Dynamics of Culture Change," in *Social Change: The Colonial Situation*, edited by Immanuel Wallerstein (New York: John Wiley and Sons, Inc., 1966); Edward H. Spicer, "Types of Contact and Processes of Change," in *Perspectives in American Indian Culture Change* (Chicago: University of Chicago Press, 1961); Social Science Research Council, "Acculturation: An Explanatory Formulation," in *Beyond the Frontier*, edited by Paul Bohannan and Fred Plog (Garden City, N.J.: Natural History Press, 1967); and Elise M. Brenner, "To Pray or Be Prey: That is the Question, Strategies for Cultural Autonomy of Massachusetts Praying Town Indians," *Ethnohistory* 27, 2 (1980): 135–52.

7. For an overview of the Dawes Act, see Frederick E. Hoxie, *A Final Promise: The Campaign to Assimilate the Indians, 1880–1920* (Lincoln: University of Nebraska Press, 1984), and Francis P. Prucha, *American Indian Policy in Crisis: Christian Reformers and the Indian, 1865–1900* (Norman: University of Oklahoma Press, 1976). On allotments, see Janet McDonnell, *The Dispossession of the American Indian, 1887–1934* (Bloomington: Indiana University Press, 1991). On education, see Robert A. Trennert, "Educating Indian Girls at Nonreservation Boarding Schools, 1878–1920," in *The American Indian, Past and Present*, edited by Roger L. Nichols, 3d ed. (New York: Alfred A. Knopf, 1986), 218–31, and Margaret C. Szasz, *Education and the American Indian* (Albuquerque: University of New Mexico Press, 1974). For a discussion of missionary activity, see Robert H. Keller, *American Protestantism and United States Indian Policy, 1869–1882* (Lincoln: University of Nebraska Press, 1983), and Francis P. Prucha, *The Churches and the Indian Schools, 1888–1912* (Lincoln: University of Nebraska Press, 1979). A general history of OIA activities is documented in Laurence F. Schmeckebier, *The Office of Indian Affairs: Its History, Activities and Organization* (Baltimore: Johns Hopkins University Press, 1927).

8. Emmerich, " 'Respect and Love,' " outlines OIA programs to acculturate Indian women. Also see Lisa Emmerich, " 'Right in the Midst of My Own People': Native American Women and the Field Matron Program," *American Indian Quarterly* 15 (Summer 1991): 201–16; Martha C. Knack, "Philene T. Hall, Bureau of Indian Affairs Field Matron: Planned Culture Change of Washakie Shoshoni Women," *Prologue: Quarterly of the United States National Archives* 22 (Summer 1990): 150–67; Helen M. Bannan, "True Womanhood on the Reservation: Field Matrons and the United States Indian Service," Working Paper No. 18 (Albuquerque: Southwest Institute for Research on Women, 1984); and Elizabeth A. McKee, "Civilizing the Indian: Field Matrons Under Hoopa Valley Agency Jurisdiction 1989–1919" (master's thesis, California State University, 1982).

9. Many contemporary Native American women have noted that their primary concerns are not combating sexism but fighting for tribal sovereignty and survival.

Of twenty-nine women who identify themselves as activists in *Native American Women: A Biographical Dictionary* (New York: Garland Press, 1993), only five call themselves feminists. Two other women state explicitly that they are at odds with American feminism, which they view as a distraction from their agenda of cultural survival. Even women who define themselves as feminists construct their identity around Indian issues. Rayna Green (*Native American Women: A Contextual Bibliography* [Bloomington: Indiana University Press, 1983], 14) writes, "For Indian feminists every women's issue is framed in the larger context of issues pertinent to Native peoples . . . the land, natural resources, water rights, and treaty guarantees." Green cautions feminist scholars of Native American women to listen to native women's definitions of their lives and not make gender the primary variable in explaining these women's experiences. M. Annette Jaimes and Theresa Halsey make the same point in "American Indian Women at the Center of Indigenous Resistance in Contemporary North America," in *The State of Native America*, edited by M. Annette Jaimes (Boston: South End Press, 1992), 311–49.

10. Two recent studies of women in Great Lakes cultures, Karen Anderson's *Chain Her By One Foot* and Carol Devens' *Countering Colonization*, argue that Indian women's responses to the assimilationist agenda were more conservative than were men's. Both authors locate the source of this traditionalism in women's loss of power and status within their culture as a result of colonization. As far as can be determined, Ute women did not suffer from this decline, and their relative ability to maintain their position in Ute culture may explain why their reactions to contact were not more conservative than men's. Most of the articles in *Ethnohistory's* special issue, *Native American Women's Responses to Christianity*, edited by Harkin and Kan, are critical of Anderson's and Devens' assertion of women's greater conservativism regarding contact with Euro-Americans.

CHAPTER I

1. S. Lyman Tyler, "The Yuta Indians Before 1880," *Western Humanities Review* 5 (Spring 1951): 157, and "The Spaniard and the Ute," *Utah Historical Quarterly* 22 (Winter 1954): 344; Donald Callaway, Joel Janetski, and Omer C. Stewart, "Ute," in *Great Basin*, edited by Warren L. d'Azevedo, vol. 11 of *Handbook of North American Indians* (hereafter cited as *HBNAI*) (Washington, D.C.: Smithsonian Institution, 1986), 336; James Jefferson, Robert W. Delaney, and Gregory C. Thompson, *The Southern Ute: A Tribal History* (Ignacio, Colo.: The Southern Ute Tribe, 1972), vii; Robert W. Delaney, *The Ute Mountain Utes* (Albuquerque: University of New Mexico Press, 1989), 5; Jan Pettit, *Utes: The Mountain People*, rev. ed. (Boulder: Johnson Books, 1990), 5; J. Donald Hughes, *American Indians in Colorado*, 2d ed. (Boulder: Pruett Publishing Company, 1987), 20. See *HBNAI* for discussions of the prehistory of the Utes.

2. Callaway, Janetski, and Stewart, "Ute," in d'Azevedo, *Great Basin*, 340–45; Jefferson, Delaney, and Thompson, *Tribal History*, vii–ix.

3. Ibid.; Opler, "Southern Ute," 124–25, 128–29. Opler estimated the population of the Southern Ute bands at 1,000, but the estimate has been revised upwards by Joseph Jorgensen in *Sun Dance Religion* (Chicago: University of Chicago Press, 1972), 37–38.

4. Carling Malouf and John M. Findlay, "Euro-American Impact Before 1870," in d'Azevedo, *Great Basin*, 500; Gloria Griffen Cline, *Exploring the Great Basin* (Westport, Conn.: Greenwood Press, Publishers, 1963), 11; Opler, "Southern Ute," 154–55, 160–61; Julian Steward, *Basin-Plateau Aboriginal Sociopolitical Groups* (Salt Lake City: University of Utah Press, 1970), 232–36; Jefferson, Delaney, and Thompson, *Tribal History*, 3–4; Carling Malouf and Arlene Malouf, "The Effects of Spanish Slavery on the Indians of the Inter-Mountain West," *Southwestern Journal of Anthropology* 1 (1945): 378–91.

5. Hughes, *American Indians in Colorado*, 42–47; Pettit, *Utes*, 99–101.

6. Jefferson, Delaney, and Thompson, *Tribal History*, 5–9, 11–12; Opler, "Southern Ute," 171–75; Hughes, *American Indians in Colorado*, 45–47. For an extensive discussion of the cultural exchange between Utes and Hispanics, see Francis Leon Swadesh, "The Southern Utes and Their Neighbors, 1877–1926" (master's thesis, University of Colorado, 1962).

7. Robert Utley, *The Indian Frontier of the American West, 1846–1890* (Albuquerque: University of New Mexico Press, 1984), 31–39, 40–63; Schmeckebier, *Office of Indian Affairs*, 26–28, 40–46.

8. Wilson Rockwell, *The Utes, A Forgotten People* (Denver: Sage Books, 1956), 64–70; P. David Smith, *Ouray, Chief of the Utes* (Ouray, Colo.: Wayfinders Press, 1986), 39; Jefferson, Delaney, and Thompson, *Tribal History*, 16–23; Gregory Coyne Thompson, *Southern Ute Lands, 1848–1899: The Creation of a Reservation*, Occasional Papers of the Center for Southwest Studies, Fort Lewis, College, Durango, Colorado, Paper No. 1, March 1972, 3–6; Richard O. Clemmer and Omer C. Stewart, "Treaties, Reservations and Claims," in d'Azevedo, *Great Basin*, 534.

9. The 1880 agreement followed the Meeker Massacre in which a band of Northern Utes rose up and killed their agent Nathan Meeker. Hughes, *American Indians in Colorado*, 66–70; Thompson, *Southern Ute Lands*, 19–22; Rockwell, *Forgotten People*, 164–73; William T. Hagan, *The Indian Rights Association* (Tucson: The University of Arizona Press, 1985), 11–20, 67–68, 127–47; House, *The Southern Ute Indians of Colorado*, 52d Cong., 1st sess., 1892, H. Rept. 1205, vol. 4, serial 3043, 1–3; C. C. Painter, "Removal of the Southern Utes" (Philadelphia: The Indian Rights Association, January 1890), 4–7, 23–27; Senate Committee on Indian Affairs, *Hearings on the Removal of the Ute Indians, January 23–25, 1890*, microfiche.

10. Thompson, *Southern Ute Lands*, 46–48; Schmeckebier, *Office of Indian Affairs*, 44–53; Paul Stuart, *The Indian Office: Growth and Development of an American Institution, 1865–1900* (Ann Arbor: University Microfilms International, 1978), 27–32; Hoxie, *Final Promise*, 1–39; McDonnell, *Dispossession*, 1–5.

11. Schmeckebier, *Office of Indian Affairs*, 78–80, 213–19; McDonnell, *Dispossession*, 87–89; Michael T. Smith, "The History of Indian Citizenship," in *The Ameri-*

can Indian, Past and Present, edited by Roger L. Nichols, 3d ed. (New York: Alfred A. Knopf, 1986), 239–41.

12. Monthly reports for 1890 are scattered throughout the Bound Letterbooks in RG 75, Records of the Consolidated Ute Agency, 44010–44013, General and Statistical, Outgoing Correspondence in Bound Letterbooks, NARA, Denver, Colorado (hereafter cited as RCUA); Charles A. Bartholomew, SUA, to CIA, 28 August 1890, RCUA, 44010; Delaney, *Ute Mountain Utes*, 75; *ARCIA*, 1886, 50.

13. Thompson, *Southern Ute Lands*, 50–51; Francis E. Leupp, "The Southern Ute," in *Annual Report of the Board of Indian Commissioners*, 1895, 1001–2 (hereafter cited as *ARBIC*); Hoxie, *Final Promise*, 249; "Act of February 20, 1895" [the Hunter Act], in Charles J. Kappler, *Indian Affairs: Laws and Treaties*, vol. 1 (Washington, D.C.: Government Printing Office, 1904), 556–57. The Fort Lewis Indian school (built in 1886) governed this jurisdiction from 1904 to 1910 when the Navajo Springs agency resumed control. After 1922 the two bureaus were classified together under the Consolidated Ute Agency, but they retained separate agencies in the two locations (Hughes, *American Indians in Colorado*, 80, 88).

14. Leupp, "Southern Ute," 1001; Thompson, *Southern Ute Lands*, 55–56. Swadesh ("Southern Utes," 123, and *Los Primeros Pobladores: Hispanic Americans of the Ute Frontier* [South Bend, Ind.: University of Notre Dame Press, 1974]) describes how relationships with Hispanic settlers in the vicinity of the reservation helped the Utes to resist assimilation programs.

15. Belle M. Brain, *The Redemption of the Red Man* (New York: Board of Home Missions of the American Presbyterian Church in the U.S.A., 1904), 99; Presbyterian Church of Colorado, *Historical Sketch of the Presbytery of Colorado* (Pueblo, Colo.: Privately Published, 1906), 41–42; "Rev. Antonio Jose Anastacio Rodriguez, 1846–1931," 108–9, typescript in Biographical Folders of Missionaries, The Presbyterian Historical Society, Philadelphia, Pennsylvania (hereafter cited as PHS Biographical Folders); David A. Day, SUA, to CIA, 7 July 1894; A. J. Rodriguez to CIA, 1 January 1902; and CIA to Rodriguez, 30 January 1902, RG 75, Special Cases 143, NARA, Washington, D.C. (hereafter cited as Special Cases 143); Browning to Day, 23 March 1897, RCUA, 44105, Education-Industries, folder "Religious Education," box 162.

16. Letters concerning the Catholic mission activity in Ignacio are found in Special Cases 143, under the following file numbers: 1903: 27145, 32182, 32183, 81863; 1906: 52012, 9464, 85665; and also in RCUA, 44012 (Burton B. Custer, SUA, to CIA, 14 June 1905; Custer to Rev. F. D. Gomez, Durango, Colorado, 7 June 1906; William D. Leonard, SUA, to Gomez, 19 November 1906; and Stephen Abbot, SUA, to Mr. Schrivner, Durango, Colorado, 28 July 1913), and 44011 (Charles F. Werner, to CIA, 17 September 1910).

17. Presbyterian Church of Colorado, *Sketch*, 41–42; "Report of A. J. Rodriguez, February 1896," typescript in PHS Biographical Folders (hereafter cited as Rodriguez Report); Brain, *Redemption*, 100–102; Rodriguez Report, October 1896; Elizabeth McAllister, "Ute Indians at Ignacio, Colorado," *The Home Mission Monthly*,

November 1902, The Presbyterian Historical Society, Philadelphia, Pennsylvania (McAllister's remark is the only reference to Utes laboring in any industry off the reservation; no agents' or inspectors' reports support this assertion).

18. "Floretta Shields: Biography," typescript in PHS Biographical Folders (hereafter cited as Shields Biography); Brain, *Redemption*, 102–3.

19. Floretta Shields, "Other Indian Stations," *The Home Mission Monthly*, November 1902, 2; E. P. Houston, "Uncivilized Utes," *The Home Mission Monthly*, February 1903, 76–77; William Peterson, Superintendent, Fort Lewis Boarding School, to CIA, 31 January 1906, RCUA, 44011; Shields Biography; Floretta Shields to Mrs. Ella Alexander Boule, Secretary, The Women's Board of Home Missions, New York, 6 June 1906, RG 305, The Presbyterian Historical Society, Philadelphia, Pennsylvania (hereafter cited as PHS RG 305); Papers of the Women's Board of Home Missions, box 3, folder 8, RG 305, The Presbyterian Historical Society, Philadelphia, Pennsylvania (hereafter cited as WBHM Papers); Opler, "Southern Ute," 191.

20. Ruth K. Barber and Edith J. Agnew, *Sowers Went Forth: The Story of Presbyterian Missions in New Mexico and Southern Colorado* (Albuquerque: Menaul Historical Library of the Southwest, 1981), 29–35, 109.

21. Presbyterian Church of Colorado, *Sketch*, 41–42; Rodriguez Report, October 1896; Brain, *Redemption*, 201; Hughes, *American Indians in Colorado*, 88; *ARCIA*, 1895, 140.

22. Frances Willard to Secretary, Women's Home Missionary Society of the Presbyterian Church, 9 September 1890; and "Women's Missionary Societies, Proposed New Departure" (reprint from *Presbyterian Banner*, 22 February 1900), WBHM Papers, box 3, folder 8.

23. "Report of the Fifteenth District," *The WCTU Messenger* 8, 1 (December 1901), Papers of the Women's Christian Temperance Union of Colorado, Western Historical Collections, Norlin Library, Boulder, Colorado (hereafter cited as WCTU Papers); *The WCTU Messenger* 9, 3 (1903), WCTU Papers; "Report of the State Executive Committee," *The WTCU Messenger*, 9, 5 (1903), WCTU Papers; Rose Adella Davidson, "On the Western Slope," *The WTCU Messenger* 11, 4 (April 1904), WCTU Papers; Barbara Leslie Epstein, *The Politics of Domesticity* (Middletown, Conn.: Wesleyan University Press, 1981), 118; Peterson to Shields, 6 October 1904, RCUA, 44013; Rose A. Davidson, "In Southern Colorado," *The WTCU Messenger* 11, 2 (1905), WTCU Papers; Miss Floretta Shields, "Work Among the Indians," Program of the 26th Annual Convention of the WCTU, 1905, WCTU Papers. Perusal of the WCTU files reveals that from 1901 to 1915 three other women attempted to bring temperance to the Utes and all failed (see *The WCTU Messenger*, 1901–15, WTCU Papers).

24. This was a representation of the book *Ten Nights in a Bar-room*, by T. S. Arthur (Chicago: M. A. Donohue & Co., n.d.).

25. Mary C. Bradford, *History and Chronology of the Colorado State Federation of Women's Clubs, 1895–1931* (Denver: CSFWC, 1932), 3, 69–77, 80–83; Mrs.

Charles W. Wiegel, "1921 Address to the State Convention," 1921 State Convention Program, Convention Programs, 1895–1935, Colorado State Federation of Women's Clubs (CSFWC) Offices, Denver, Colorado (hereafter cited as CSFWC Convention Programs); Yearbook Files, CSFWC Offices, Denver, Colorado (hereafter cited as CSFWC Yearbook Files); Minutes of the Executive Board of the CSFWC, 1914–1922, CSFWC Offices, Denver, Colorado; General Federation of Women's Clubs, *Sixty Years of Achievement: 1890–1950* (New York: The General Federation of Women's Clubs, 1950), 10; Mrs. Charles W. Wiegel, "Indian Welfare," *The Colorado Clubwoman*, March 1926, 9; September 1926, 6; January 1927, 8, CSFWC Offices, Denver, Colorado.

26. Bradford, *History*, 80; CIA to Wiegel, 2 March 1932, CCF-CU, 154–55399.

27. Wiegel to McKean, 27 November 1925; McKean to Wiegel, 18 January 1926; Wiegel to McKean, 18 January 1926; CIA to Wiegel, n.d.; McKean to CIA, 21 April 1926; and CIA to Wiegel, 30 April 1926, RCUA, 44014, General and Statistical, Policy and Administration, box 1.

28. McKean to CIA, 21 April 1926; and CIA to Wiegel, 30 April 1926, RCUA, 44014, box 1; CIA to Wiegel, 30 March 1927, CCF-CU, 156–70300; Mrs. C. W. Wiegel, "The Ute's Last Stand"; Wiegel to Senator Burton B. Wheeler and Senator Lynn J. Frazier, 24 February 1931, Records of the U.S. Senate, RG 46, Special File 224, SEN83A-F9, box 50, no. 10, RG 75, Records of the Bureau of Indian Affairs, NARA, Washington, D.C. (hereafter cited as Senate File 224); Wiegel to CIA, n.d.; and CIA to Wiegel, 31 January 1927, Senate File 244; Wiegel to CIA, June 1928; CIA to Wiegel, 28 June 1928; and H. H. Fiske, "Investigation of the Death of Joe Salt by Max Buffalo," 3 June 1927, CCF-CU, 821–4335; CIA to Wiegel, 16 September 1927; and Wiegel to CIA, 21 September 1927, Senate File 224.

29. "Committee of Women's Clubs Looks After Indians," *Rocky Mountain News*, 23 November 1925, RCUA, 44014, box 1.

30. This incident will be discussed in more detail in chapter 5. Fiske to CIA, 11 May 1927; and Fiske to J. F. Garland, Chief Inspector, Interior Department, 22 May 1927, CCF-CU, 154–44331; Roy Nash and H. J. Hagerman, "Report of Conditions at the Southern Ute Agency, 1931–1933," in 3 parts, CCF-CU, 154–55399 (hereafter cited as Nash-Hagerman Report), pt. 1, passim; Charles J. Rhodes, CIA, to Secretary of the Interior, 27 February 1932; Rhodes to Wiegel, 2 March 1932; Wiegel to Ray Lyman Wilbur, Secretary of the Interior, 11 March 1932; Wiegel to CIA, 5 July 1932; Wiegel to CIA, 12 August 1932; Nash-Hagerman Report, pt. 3; and Wiegel to CIA, 12 August 1932, CCF-CU, 832–40017; CSFWC Yearbook Files, 1925–62 (listing officers for every year).

31. Wiegel to Burton B. Wheeler and Lynn J. Frazier, U.S. Senators, 24 February 1931, Senate File 224; CSFWC Yearbook Files; 1932 State Convention Program, CSFWC Convention Programs; Mrs. Edward Bain, *History and Chronology of the Colorado State Federation of Women's Clubs, 1895–1955* (Denver: CSFWC, 1956), 156.

CHAPTER 2

1. Chipeta, wife of Chief Ouray, accompanied him to Washington. See Pettit, *Utes*, 123, 128. For all-male councils on policy, see Henry Page, SUA, to CIA, 12 December 1879; CIA to Christian Stollsteimer, SUA, 19 August 1885, 10 and 21 January 1886; CIA to Thomas McCunniff, SUA, 14 July 1888; and CIA to Stollsteimer, 21 January 1886, RCUA, 44014, folder "Tribal Relations," box 1.

2. *Regulations of the Indian Department* (Washington, D.C.: Government Printing Office, 1884), 37–39; *Rulebook Governing the Court of Indian Offenses* (Washington, D.C.: The Department of the Interior, 1883), 4, RCUA, 44016, General and Statistical, Reports, Enrollment, box 7 (hereafter cited as *Rulebook*).

3. Callaway, Janetski, and Stewart, "Ute," in d'Azevedo, *Great Basin*, 338; Opler, "Southern Ute," 123–30, 160, 169–70; Julian Steward, *Basin-Plateau*, 13–33, 44–56; James Goss, "Ute Myth as a Cultural Charter," paper presented at the Great Basin Anthropological Conference, Reno, Nevada, 1990, 1, and "Ute Language, Kin, Myth, and Nature: A Multidimensional Folk Taxonomy," *Anthropological Linguistics* 9, 9 (1966): 8. For a discussion of how the relative lack of centralized power in hunting and gathering societies affects women, see Maltz and Archambault, "Gender," 230–49.

4. Opler, "Southern Ute," 124–30; Hughes, *American Indians in Colorado*, 29–30.

5. Opler, "Southern Ute," 162–66.

6. Ibid., 166.

7. Ibid., 136, 141–42; Callaway, Janetski, and Stewart, "Ute," in d'Azevedo, *Great Basin*, 334, 354; Hughes, *American Indians in Colorado*, 28–29; Goss, "Ute Myth," 2; Ake Hultkrantz, "Mythology and Religious Concepts," in d'Azevedo, *Great Basin*, 637; Robert H. Lowie, "Shoshonean Tales," *Journal of American Folklore* 37, 143 (1924): 1–91.

8. Opler, "Southern Ute," 137, 141–44. Several cases of murder that specifically mention medicine men are found in OIA files. See Bartholomew to CIA, RCUA, 44010; Harwood Hall to C. A. Bonfils, 22 June 1904, RCUA, 44012; "Report of H. J. Sticken, Moses Hamlin, Murder Victim," 24 September 1929, CCF-CU, 48276–175; RCUA, 44014, folder "Murder Cases, 1878–1911," box 3; Opler, "Southern Ute," 139–40; Callaway, Janetski, and Stewart, "Ute," in d'Azevedo, *Great Basin*, 354.

9. See RCUA, 44017, Tribal and Administrative Documents, folders "Regulations and Circulars by Subject Heading," boxes 10–11; *ARCIA*, 1886, 50; Monthly Report of Charles Bartholomew, SUA, to CIA, 9 April 1890, RCUA, 44010; Monthly Report of David A. Day, SUA, to CIA, 31 March 1894, Letters Received by the Office of Indian Affairs, 1894: 12999, RG 75, Records of the Bureau of Indian Affairs, NARA, Washington, D.C. (hereafter cited as LROIA); "Act of February 20, 1895" [the Hunter Act], 53d Cong., 3d sess., 1895, RCUA, 44017, folder "Land," box 11; D. M. Browning, CIA, to Meredith H. Kidd, Southern Ute Allotting Com-

mission (SUAC), 20 April 1895, RCUA, 44017, folder "Land," box 11. Colorado voters had approved women's suffrage in 1893. Carl Ubbelohde, Maxine Benson, and Duane A. Smith, *A Colorado History*, 6th ed. (Boulder: Pruett Publishing Company, 1988), 232–33.

10. Browning to SUAC, 20 April 1895, RCUA, 44017, folder "Land," box 11.

11. *ARCIA*, 1895, 140.

12. G. B. Perry, SUA, to CIA, 10 April 1899, Southern Ute Agency Letters, 5 March 1899 to 26 July 1899, Microfilm Collection, I-053, roll 1, Center for Southwest Studies, Fort Lewis College, Durango, Colorado (hereafter cited as SUA Letters).

13. Bartholomew to CIA, 28 August 1890, RCUA, 44010.

14. Bartholomew to CIA, 10 May and 8 June 1891, RCUA, 44010.

15. "Resolution of the Southern Ute Council," 5 November 1896, RCUA, 44017, folder "Resolution . . . ," box 10; Werner to CIA, 20 February 1911, RCUA, 44011; Werner to CIA, 17 April 1912, Central Classified Files, Southern Ute Agency, 54628–310, RG 75, Records of the Bureau of Indian Affairs, NARA, Washington, D.C. (hereafter cited as CCF-SU); Charles McChesney, SUA, to CIA, 10 February 1913, CCF-SU, 35457–916; Walter Runke, SUA, to CIA, 10 February 1913, RCUA, 44011; "To the Indian Commissioner," 15 November 1916, RCUA, 44013; McKean to CIA, 15 May 1919, CCF-SU, 92877–154; Perkins and Perkins, Attorneys at Law, Durango, Colorado, to CIA, 5 April 1922, CCF-SU, 29201–155 (quotation is from the petition of 1916). Edward E. McKean, SUA, to CIA, 22 March 1926, RCUA, 44017, folder "Complaints, Charges Against McKean, BIA, 1925," box 10; McKean to CIA, 8 and 9 December 1925, CCF-CU, 70300–056.

16. Mary Baker Pena to CIA, 9 November 1925, "Selected Documents Relating to the Ute Indians, 1881–1939," CCF-CU, Microfilm, roll 4, photocopy held at Center for Southwest Studies, Fort Lewis College, Durango, Colorado (hereafter cited as Selected Documents).

17. McKean to T. B. Roberts, Special Inspector, 8 December 1925; and T. B. Roberts to CIA, 9 December 1925, Selected Documents.

18. *ARCIA*, 1880, 17; Page to CIA, 5 November 1880, RCUA, 44010; Page to CIA, 3 December 1880, 2 January 1881, and 9 February 1881, RCUA, 44010.

19. Warren Patten, SUA, to CIA and Henry M. Teller, Secretary of the Interior, 16 March 1883, RCUA, 44010; Teller to Patten, 23 March 1883, LROIA, 1883: 5510; William B. Clark, SUA, to CIA, 21 November 1884; Bartholomew to Louis Morgan, Superintendent, Fort Lewis School, 22 October 1892; Bartholomew to CIA, 21 November 1892; H. B. Freeman, SUA, to CIA, 27 July 1893; and David A. Day to CIA, 29 November 1894, RCUA, 44010; William Peterson, Superintendent, Fort Lewis School, to Mrs. Virginia McClurg, Colorado Springs, Colorado, 3 October 1904, RCUA, 44012.

20. Patten to CIA, 25 May and 8 August 1883, 9 October 1884; Clark to CIA, 20 October and 17 November 1884, RCUA, 44010; Stollsteimer to CIA, 28 December 1887, LROIA, 1887: 566.

21. *ARCIA*, 1887, 15.

22. Stollsteimer to CIA, 28 December 1887, LROIA, 1887: 566; the OIA also established the Allen day school in 1909 and the Ute Mountain boarding school in 1915. Milton Hoyt, "The Development of Education Among the Southern Utes" (Ph.D. diss., University of Colorado, Boulder, 1967), 335–48; Hughes, *American Indians in Colorado*, 85–89; *ARCIA*, 1886, 49; Stollsteimer to CIA, 28 December 1887, LROIA, 1887: 566; *ARCIA*, 1890, 23; 1891, 22.

23. *ARCIA*, 1901, 204; 1902, 180.

24. The annual reports for each year from 1904 to 1920 note the Utes' pleasure with the school. Also see Hoyt, "Development," 347–49. Hoyt notes that school enrollments were filled to capacity—about seventy pupils on average—but that average daily attendance during the first two decades of the twentieth century was about fifty-nine.

25. Joseph O. Smith, SUA, to CIA, 25 November 1902, RCUA, 44012.

26. "Education Circular No. 130, 15 January 1906," RCUA, 44016, folder "Education Circulars, 1878–1907," box 11; Peterson to Smith, 24 October 1904, RCUA, 44010.

27. Peterson to CIA, 28 November 1904, RCUA, 44101, Supplies; Peterson to CIA, 6 October and 21 December 1904; 7 April and 30 May 1905; and 31 January and 28 May 1906, RCUA, 44010.

28. Personnel file of Floretta Shields, PHS Biographical Folders; PHS RG 305; WBHM Papers; Peterson to CIA, 31 January 1906, RCUA, 44011; "An Observer," and "Uncivilized Utes," *The Home Mission Monthly*, February 1903, 75.

29. "Education Circular No. 62, 17 January 1902," RCUA, 44016, folder "Education Circulars, 1878–1907," box 11; the individual Indian files contain statements to this effect in nearly all family files (see RCUA, 44015, General and Statistical, Status File of Indians, boxes 4–6).

30. *Regulations*, 1884, 37.

31. Ibid.

32. Francis Weaver, SUA, to CIA, 14 March 1878; 17 March 1878, RCUA, 44014, folder "Establishment of the Los Pinos Agency—1887–78," box 2.

33. Opler, "Southern Ute," 129–30.

34. Weaver to CIA, 17 March 1878, RCUA, 44014, folder "Establishment."

35. Weaver to CIA, 27 April 1878, RCUA, 44014, folder "Establishment."

36. Opler, "Southern Ute," 128–29, 169. Richard Clemmer, who did fieldwork at Southern Ute in the late 1970s and early 1980s, noted that at one time a faction of women withdrew from the tribal council and formed their own council in order to protest the policies of the main body. This council had no official authority but nevertheless continued to meet for some time (personal communication, 1990).

37. Monthly Report of Agent Weaver, 12 March 1878, Letters Received by the Office of Indian Affairs, The Colorado Superintendency, M234, roll 209, 1878, RG 75, Records of the Bureau of Indian Affairs, NARA, Denver, Colorado (hereafter cited as LROIA-CS); *ARCIA*, 1878, 17.

38. Opler, "Southern Ute," 188–90; Joseph G. Jorgensen, "Ghost Dance, Bear Dance, and Sun Dance," in d'Azevedo, *Great Basin*, 660–61.

39. Omer C. Stewart, "The Peyote Religion," in d'Azevedo, *Great Basin*, 673–81; Opler, "Southern Ute," 190–94.

40. Jorgensen, *Sun Dance*, 64–65, and "Ghost Dance," in d'Azevedo, *Great Basin*, 231–43, 665–67. For testimonies of modern Ute women participants in Peyotism and the Sun Dance, see Pettit, *Utes*, 152–57. The story of a woman's Sun Dance comes from Oral Histories, FLC.

41. Thomas Jefferson Morgan, CIA, "Field Matrons," *ARCIA*, 1892, 101; Mrs. Cora Dunn, Superintendent, Rainy Mountain School, Anadarko, Oklahoma, "More Systematic Training Along Industrial Lines," *ARCIA*, 1900, 452; Joan Jacobs Brumberg, "Zenanas and Girlless Villages: The Ethnology of America Evangelical Women, 1870–1910," *Journal of American History* 69, 2 (1982): 347–71; Barbara Welter, " 'She Hath Done What She Could': Protestant Women's Missionary Careers in Nineteenth-Century America," *American Quarterly* (Winter 1978): 624–38. See also, Barbara Welter, "The Feminization of American Religion: 1800–1860," in *Clio's Consciousness Raised*, edited by Mary S. Hartman and Lois Banner (New York: Harper & Row Publishers, 1974), 137–57.

42. The agreement of 1880 provided individual allotments of land for the Utes in order to encourage farming. This process of allotment preceded the Dawes Act of 1887 that broke up the reservation into individual allotments. *ARCIA*, 1880, 18; 1881, 23; 1882, 18; 1883, 20; 1885, 564; 1890, 23, 498; 1893, 133. Population figures for the period 1892–93 show 510 adult men. *ARCIA*, 1893, 132–133; 1895, 140, 566.

43. *ARCIA*, 1896, 204; Burton B. Custer, SUA, to CIA, 10 June 1905, RCUA, 44012; Charles F. Werner, SUA, to CIA, 18 June 1909, CCF-SU, 127–4906; *Statistics Accompanying the Agents' Annual Narrative Report*, 1912, 1, RCUA, 44016, box 8 (hereafter cited as *SANR*); *ARCIA*, 1918, 3; 1920, 3; summary of the statistical data in the agents' annual reports from 1885 to 1925 found in both the serial sets and the files at the RCUA. The years 1906–10 are not available. "Industrial Survey, 1929," RCUA, 44105, box 162; quotation is from "Report of Special Inspector J. H. Fleming, 3 April 1915," CCF-SU, 84217 (hereafter cited as Fleming Report); "Report of Special Inspector L. F. Michael, 11 April 1918," Section I, CCF-SU, 32403 (hereafter cited as Michael Report); "Industrial Survey, 1929," RCUA, 44105, box 162.

44. *ARCIA*, 1880, 18; 1881, 23; RCUA, 44103, Supplies, Military Service, Health and Social Relations, folders "Epidemics, Contagious Diseases, 1877–1926" and "Sanitary Reports: Quarterly Reports for 1890–92," boxes 155–56; Bartholomew's comments on accusations of witchcraft, Bartholomew to CIA, 10 May 1890, RCUA, 44010; "Report of Elsie E. Newton, Supervisor for Home Economics, February 1915," CCF-SU, 150 (hereafter cited as Newton Report, 1915).

45. L. D. C. Atkins, CIA, "To All United States Indian Agents, 29 October 1887," RCUA, 44014, folder "Correspondence Between Northern and Southern Utes," box 1.

46. Ibid., passim (quotation is from William D. Leonard, SUA, addressee unread-

able, 14 January 1907, RCUA 44012); Peterson to Custer, 17 November 1905; Leonard to CIA, 10 September 1906; Peterson to SUA, 7 April 1905, and to Custer, 19 and 22 May 1905, RCUA, 44013.

CHAPTER 3

1. Hoxie, *Final Promise*, 77, 168–70, chap. 6; Schmeckebier, *Office of Indian Affairs*, 69, 252–54, 196–97, 467–70; "Report of Chester B. Davis, Supervisor of Farming, 3 April 1913," CCF-SU, 448810–916 (hereafter cited as Davis Report). OIA rations policy underscored the ideal of women's economic dependence. When gender distinctions appear, it is clear that able-bodied women received far more rations than did men (see *SANR*, 1911–25, RCUA, 44016, box 8); Francis Weaver, SUA, to CIA, 14 February 1877, RCUA, 44016, folder "Agents' Reports, 1877–1905," box 7; *ARCIA*, 1879, 17; 1881, 23; 1882, 97; 1891, 227.

2. *ARCIA*, 1883, 20; 1885, 15; 1890, 226–27; 1891, 232; 1894, 129.

3. Davis Report; Seldon K. Emerson, Agency Farmer, to Walter Runke, SUA, 18 November 1913, RCUA, 44011; *SANR*, RCUA, 44016, box 8. See also *ARCIA*, 1910, 5; 1911, 13; 1912, 13; 1913, 19; 1914, 9–10; West to CIA, 4 October 1916, RCUA, 44013; Michael Report; E. J. Peacore, SUA, to CIA, 11 June 1928, CCF-CU, 70300–056; Peacore to CIA, 16 April and 18 October 1929, CCF-CU, 16729–910.

4. Charles F. Werner, SUA, to CIA, 10 February 1913, CCF-SU, 35457–916; Davis Report; Werner to CIA, 7 June 1912; W. B. Fry, ex–Supervisor of Farming, to CIA, 13 January 1913; and Charles E. McChesney, SUA, to CIA, 10 February 1913, CCF-SU, 35457–916; "Report of Special Indian Agent W. W. McConihe, Southern Ute Reservation, 15 August 1916," CCF-SU, 89503–910, 20–37 (hereafter cited as McConihe Report); "Report of Special Inspector P. J. Lonergan, 1921," CCF-SU, 47243–310; "Report of Special Indian Agent H. H. Fiske, 27 September 1927," CCF-CU, 40973–806 (hereafter cited as Fiske Report) Ute Water Rights are found in "Act of March 3, 1905," in Kappler, *Indian Affairs*, 1: 157; *ARCIA*, 1910, M1011, 3; McKean to CIA, 7 June 1918, CCF-SU, 32403–910; "Inspection Report of John C. Atwater, Southern Ute Agency, 27–31 January 1922," CCF-CU, 10473–910 (hereafter cited as Atwater Report).

5. Werner to CIA, 8 February 1909, CCF-SU, 55824–824; "Report of Harwood Hall, Supervisor of Indian Schools, 26 August 1909," Section C, CCF-SU, 70275–4-09–811 (hereafter cited as Hall Report). Robert A. Trennert, "From Carlisle to Phoenix: The Rise and Fall of the Outing System, 1878–1930," *Pacific Historical Review* 52 (August 1983), 267; Werner to CIA, 6 July 1911, CCF-SU, 48346–920; *SANR*, 1911–25, RCUA, 44016, box 8; "Indian Employment at Agency, etc.," RCUA, 44105, folders "Utes, 1879–1939," and "Non-Utes, 1908–38," box 16; Open Market Purchases, 1877–1897, RCUA, 44020, Finance and Accounts, Receipts for Goods, folders "Vouchers," boxes 16–17; Correspondence File, RCUA, 44014, folder "Fairs and Expositions: Indian Attendance, 1882–1917," box 1.

6. D. M. Browning, CIA, to SUAC, 15 August 1895, RCUA, 44017, folder "Land: Regulations and Circulars, 1887–1942," box 11; Browning to Henry Page, SUA, 8 July 1881, RCUA, 44017, folder "Land," box 11.

7. Schmeckebier, *Office of Indian Affairs*, 257–58. Schmeckebier quotes the Board of Indian Commissioners' 1919 ruling on the subject of marriage and divorce laws. Cato Sells, CIA, to McKean, 28 December 1917, CCF-SU, 104064. The Dawes Act originally provided for citizenship in twenty-five years when the trust period for the land patents expired and Indians were issued fee patents for their lands (see Public No. 43, RCUA, 44017, folder "Land," box 11). In 1905, however, the U.S. Supreme Court ruled, in *Matter of Heff*, that Indians became citizens at the beginning of the trust period when they accepted allotments (see McDonnell, *Dispossession*, 88–89). In 1906 the Dawes Act was amended to postpone again the granting of citizenship for twenty-five years but to allow the secretary of the interior to grant patents to competent Indians (see M. Smith, "History," 232–41). The result of these actions was a terrible alienation of Indian lands.

8. *General Statutes, State of Colorado, 1883* (Denver: Colorado Times Stream and Publishing House, 1884), 694–95; Sells to McKean, 13 June 1918, CCF-SU, 104064.

9. Allotment Tract Book, Bureau of Land Management (BLM) Office, Denver, Colorado. Southern Ute Census Records, Omer Stewart Collection, Series II, box 4, Western Historical Collections, Norlin Library, University of Colorado, Boulder, Colorado (hereafter cited as Stewart Collection). Southern Ute Death Records, Tri-Ethnic Files, Western Historical Collections, Norlin Library, University of Colorado, Boulder, Colorado (hereafter cited as Tri-Ethnic Files). Omer Stewart's Personal Papers, Western Historical Collections, Norlin Library, University of Colorado, Boulder, Colorado (hereafter cited as Stewart Personal Papers). Runke to Mr. Guy Tucker, Durango, Colorado, 6 January 1914, RCUA, 44012.

10. Opler, "Southern Ute," 151, 128–29.

11. William D. Leonard, SUA, to CIA, 6 November 1906, RCUA, 44012; Runke to CIA, 21 March 1914, RCUA, 44011; Alphabetical Status Files of Indians 1879–1939, Baker File, RCUA, 44015.

12. "Petition for the Sale of Land by the Original Allottee, Benjamin North," CCF-SU, 310–136344; Walter West, SUA, to CIA, 29 September 1916, and 9 March 1917; West to CIA, 9 March 1917, RCUA, 44013.

13. Opler, "Southern Ute," 137–38.

14. Ibid., 133–34.

15. Burton B. Custer, SUA, "To All it May Concern," 6 June 1905, RCUA, 44013.

16. West to Daisy Spencer Baker, Pagosa Junction, Colorado, 6 June 1916, RCUA, 44013; Daisy Spencer Baker to CIA, 26 November 1917, CCF-SU, 310–104064.

17. McKean to CIA, 26 November 1917, CCF-SU, 310–104064; CIA to McKean, 28 December 1917, RCUA, 44015, Baker File.

18. Daisy S. Baker to McKean, 21 January 1918, RCUA, 44015, Baker File.

19. McKean to Daisy S. Baker, 22 January, 15 February, 11 March 1918, RCUA, 44015, Baker File; Daisy S. Baker to McKean, 15 March 1918, RCUA, 44015, Baker File; CIA to McKean, 15 June 1918, RCUA, 44015, Baker File.

20. Heirship Report of James Baker, 1927, RCUA, 44015, Baker File.

21. Opler, "Southern Ute," 137–40; Hultkrantz, "Mythology," in d'Azevedo, *Great Basin*, 637–39; James Goss, "Ute Myth," 2, 6; John Wesley Powell, *Anthropology of the Numu: John Wesley Powell's Manuscripts on the Numu Peoples of Western North America, 1868–1880*, edited by Don Fowler and Catherine Fowler, Smithsonian Contributions to Anthropology No. 14 (Washington, D.C.: Smithsonian Institution Press, 1971), 44–48, 88–89; Robert H. Lowie, "Shoshonean Tales," 28–30; Anne Smith, *Ute Tales* (Salt Lake City: University of Utah Press, 1992), passim.

22. Jorgensen, "Ghost Dance," in d'Azevedo, *Great Basin*, 662–63. In postcontact times the primary focus of the dance shifted from sexual and hunting success to healing and well-being. This was a response to the stress of contact.

23. *Rulebook*, 8; the agents' annual reports to the CIA included a "Law and Order" section in which virtually every agent from 1906 to 1929 told how he stressed the need for legal marriages. *General Statutes, State of Colorado*, 397–98, 244. The 1891 statute book elaborated on these provisions but did not alter them in any way (see *General Statutes, State of Colorado*, 1891 [Denver: Colorado Times Stream Printing and Publishing House, 1892], 1035–50).

24. McKean to CIA, 26 November 1917, CCF-SU, 104064–310.

25. I am grateful to Richard White for helping me clarify this concept (see Richard White, *The Middle Ground: Indians, Empires, and Republics in the Great Lakes Region, 1650–1815* [Cambridge, U.K.: Cambridge University Press, 1991]).

26. *ARCIA*, 1911, M1011, 9; see the education sections in *ARCIA*, 1910–25, M1011, and RCUA, 44016, boxes 7–8, for a year-by-year summary of educational programs. For information on gender-based education for earlier years, see "School Curriculum, Textbooks, Teaching Methods, 1889–1926," box 162, and "Pupil Reports, 1887–1910," box 160, both in RCUA, 44105; Annual Report, Southern Ute Boarding School (SUB), 17 August 1903, RCUA, 44011; Leonard to CIA, 3, 19, and 24 September 1906, RCUA, 44012; Circular No. 3, 9 January 1878, RCUA, 44016, folder "Education Circulars, 1878–1907," box 11; William Peterson, Supervisor of Indian Schools, to CIA, 18 February 1912, CCF-SU, 36577–806 (hereafter cited as Peterson Report). "Report of Frederick Snyder, Superintendent of Indian Schools, April 1916," CCF-SU, 374126–800, and June 1917, CCF-SU, 65553–806 (hereafter cited as Snyder Report). "Report of C. H. Asbury, Special Indian Agent, 22 December 1916," CCF-SU, 150 (hereafter cited as Asbury Report). Michael Report, Section III, CCF-SU, 32401–310; Albert B. Reagan, Principal, SUB, to CIA, 19 October 1916, CCF-SU, 111207–810; Newton Report, 1915; Elsie E. Newton, "Report on the Southern Ute Boarding School, 3 July 1918," CCF-SU, 150–57745 (hereafter cited as Newton Report, 1918).

27. Indian children were initially paid for their work. In 1901, however, OIA

Commissioner W. A. Jones issued a circular disallowing this practice. In his reasoning, the OIA was providing civilization for the Indian children and "this is payment enough" (Schmeckebier, *Office of Indian Affairs*, 218; OIA Circular Number 60, 20 December 1901, RCUA, 44016; *SANR*, 1910–25, RCUA, 44016, box 8, 23, 24).

28. West to E. D. Smith, County Agricultural Agent, Durango, Colorado, 29 December 1916, RCUA, 44013; *ARCIA*, 1918, 17; McKean to CIA, 20 February 1926, RCUA, 44103, Supplies, Military Service, Health and Social Relations, folder "Clubs, Sports, Recreation," box 154; CIA to McKean, 11 March 1926, CCF-CU, 22809–823; William Moyer, Teacher, SUB, to McKean, 19 March 1926, CCF-CU, 22809–823.

29. Leonard to CIA, 19 September 1906, RCUA, 44011; Mrs. Merial Dorchester, Special Agent, Indian School Service, "Suggestions From the Field," *ARCIA*, 1891, pt. 1, 542; West to CIA, 25 May 1916, RCUA, 44013.

30. For statements of the purposes of education for Indian women, see *ARCIA*, 1914, 7; Werner, *ARCIA*, 1911, 11. For requests for Indian servant girls, see Peterson to Mr. T. B. Carpenter, Salt Lake City, Utah, 22 July 1905; Peterson to Aura B. Work, Panguitch, Utah, 22 July 1905; and Peterson, letters to various farmers in Colorado, 21 January, 13 and 24 May, 12 and 24 June, 22 July, and 22 September 1905, RCUA, 44013; Spear to Mrs. O. E. Noland, Mancos, Colorado, 9 April 1906, RCUA, 44013; Spear to Guillet Brothers, Cortez, Colorado, 14 May 1906, RCUA, 44013; Spear to Mr. and Mrs. P. H. Head, Farmington, New Mexico, 14 April 1906, RCUA, 44013.

31. Spear to Miss Lucy Head, Mancos, Colorado, 9 July 1906; and Spear to George Carr, 9 July 1906, RCUA, 44013.

32. Spear to Mr. P. H. Head, Farmington, New Mexico, 23 July 1906, RCUA, 44013.

33. Spear to Mr. J. J. Shideler, 15 August 1906, RCUA, 44013; see Spear to Carr, 23 July 1906; Spear to E. H. Menefee, Mancos, Colorado, 24 July 1906; and Spear to Carr, 27 July 1906, RCUA, 44013.

34. Peterson to Mr. C. T. Smith, Breen, Colorado, 24 June 1905; and Peterson to J. J. Snideler, Breen, Colorado, 26 September 1906, RCUA, 44013, mention the women's discontent. Abbott to CIA, 18 June 1913, CCF-SU, 78577–826 (quotation from West to Mrs. Pearl [water damaged, name and date unreadable]), RCUA, 44012.

35. West to Nancy Shoshone, date unreadable; and West to Mr. Frederick Snyder, Superintendent, Santa Fe Indian School, 17 August 1916, RCUA, 44012; West to The Arlington Hotel, Pagosa Springs, Colorado, 23 June 1917, Shoshone Student File, Records of the Santa Fe Indian School, Center for Southwest Studies, Fort Lewis College, Durango, Colorado (hereafter cited as Shoshone Student File); West to Nancy Shoshone, 4 January 1917, RCUA, 44013; Nancy Shoshone, Durango, Colorado, to McKean, 1 May 1918, Shoshone Student File.

36. Nancy Shoshone to Snyder, 8 January 1917, Shoshone Student File.

37. Nancy Shoshone to West, 20 February 1917, Shoshone Student File.

38. Nancy Shoshone to West, 8 January 1917; Snyder to West, 17 March 1917; and Shoshone to Snyder, 11 May 1917, Shoshone Student File.

39. Shoshone to Snyder, 11 August 1917; and Shoshone to Mrs. Burrows, Santa Fe, New Mexico, 20 August 1917, Shoshone Student File; Shoshone to McKean, 1 May 1918; McKean to Shoshone, 2 May 1918; and Shoshone to McKean, 13 June 1918, Shoshone Student File.

40. Shoshone to McKean, 1 May 1918; McKean to Shoshone, 2 May 1918; and Shoshone to McKean, 13 June 1918, Shoshone Student File.

41. Shoshone and Southern Paiute women in mining towns of Nevada during the same period were forced to support themselves as laundresses and domestic servants for families in the mining camps. These women seem to have participated in the labor market to a much greater extent than did Southern Ute women. See Martha Knack, "Newspaper Accounts of Indian Women in Southern Nevada Mining Towns, 1870–1900," *Journal of California and Great Basin Anthropology* 8, 1 (1986): 83–98.

42. *ARCIA*, 1877, 43; 1878, 15; 1880, 17; 1881, 23; 1882, 18; 1883, 20; LROIA-CS, M234, rolls 211, 212, passim; also LROIA, 1881: 1018, 9082, 9085, 11550; 1885: 9223, 16240, 9837, 13843; 1889: 26709, 29137, 29138, 25065. R. E. H. Crofton, Commander, Ft. Wingate, Arizona, to Assistant Adjutant General, Santa Fe, New Mexico, 28 July 1883, RCUA, 44014, folder "Depredation Suits," box 3; Oral Histories, FLC.

43. Werner, *ARCIA*, 1910, 6; *SANR*, 1911–25, RCUA, 44016, box 8, 29–31. Albert J. Floyd giving testimony before the Senate Committee on Indian Affairs, quoted in Senate, *Survey of Conditions of the Indians in the United States* (Washington, D.C.: Government Printing Office, 1931), 10, 609–10, 704 (hereafter cited as Senate Indian Survey, 1931).

44. Snyder Report, 1917; Thomas Jefferson Morgan, CIA, *ARCIA*, 1892, 101; quotation from *ARCIA*, 1919, 18; Seldon K. Emerson, Agency Farmer, to Runke, 18 November 1913, RCUA, 44011; Newton Report, 1915; Snyder Report, 1917; Senate Indian Survey, 1931, 10681–96.

45. Peacore to CIA, 2 February 1934, Wheeler-Howard Act Files, RG 75, 1011, A894, Records of the Bureau of Indian Affairs, NARA, Washington, D.C.; Senate Indian Survey, 1931, 10681–96. Care of animals in the period prior to the reservation was not gender based. Pre-reservation Utes owned horses and dogs. Men generally owned and cared for the horses, but women could own and tend them as well—and dogs were not owned or tended by anyone (Lowie, "Notes," 215, 249; Pettit, *Utes*, 18, 21; Richard O. Clemmer, personal communication, 1990).

46. David Rich Lewis, *Neither Wolf nor Dog: American Indians, Environment and Agrarian Change* (New York: Oxford University Press, 1994); Douglas R. Hurt, *Indian Agriculture in America: Prehistory to the Present* (Lawrence: University Press of Kansas, 1987).

47. Opler, "Southern Ute," 125, 135; Employee Vouchers, 30 November 1879, RCUA, 44016, folder "Employee Changes, 1877–79," box 12; Opler, "Southern Ute," 137–40; *SANR*, 1919, RCUA, 44016, box 8, 34.

48. C. A. Churchill, Superintendent, Jicarilla Agency, to Charles E. McChesney, SUA, 4 March 1911; and E. O. Greene, Superintendent, Jicarilla Agency to Southern Ute, 18 October 1913, RCUA, 44015, B. File.

49. For a detailed explanation of the field matrons program see chapter 4. Agent West notes that A. B. got her job because of her schooling (*ARCIA*, 1916, 16, M1011). For information on Susan, see Hughes, *American Indians in Colorado*, 68; and Marshall Sprague, *Massacre: The Tragedy at White River* (Lincoln: University of Nebraska Press, 1980), 88–89, 259, 277–79, 284, 292. For Indian women as intermediaries, see Clara Sue Kidwell, "Indian Women as Cultural Mediators," *Ethnohistory* 39, 2 (1992): 97–107. A detailed description of Ute-Hispanic intermarriage is found in Francis Leon Swadesh, "Southern Utes" (for remarks on women as traders, see 164–65).

50. *ARCIA*, 1916, 7, M1011. Morris's efficiency was a matter of debate between Agent West and OIA inspector W. W. McConihe (see chapter 4 for this disagreement). *ARCIA*, 1916–17, Statistical Section, Employment, 56, RCUA, 44016, box 7; West to CIA, 24 January 1917, RCUA, 44013; West to Snyder, 4 October 1917, RCUA, 44015, B. File.

51. Pettit (*Utes*, chapters 3 and 4) describes Ute material culture in detail. For a discussion of the effect of the reservation on Indian artwork, including that of the Utes, see Richard Conn, *A Persistent Vision: Art of the Reservation Days* (Seattle: University of Washington Press, for Denver Art Museum, 1986).

52. Werner, *ARCIA*, 1910, 6; *ARCIA*, 1911–25, 34.

53. See Peacore's letters in the "Arts and Crafts" folder of RCUA, 44105, box 162.

54. Both the Denver Art Museum and the Colorado Historical Society have numerous Ute artifacts from the early reservation era, which may never have been considered by the Southern Ute agents. When Mrs. Collier (no relation to CIA John Collier who instituted the 1934 Indian Reorganization Act) surveyed Southern Ute artisans in 1934 for the Indian Arts Project, she found fourteen bead workers, two basket makers, and one silversmith on the reservation (see Mrs. Charles Collier, "Survey of Indian Arts and Crafts, April 1934," RCUA, 44105, folder "Arts and Crafts," box 162); also see Bradford, *History*, 3, 69–77, 80.

55. Mrs. Charles Wiegel to McKean, 18 January 1926; McKean to Wiegel, 21 January 1926; and Wiegel to McKean, 5 February, 6 April, and 8 May 1926, RCUA, 44014, box 1.

56. Requests for "show" Indians are found in RCUA, 44014, folder "Fairs and Expositions, 1882–1917," box 1; in 44012, 3 June 1911, and 30 June, 11 July, and 16 August 1913; and in 44013, 4 October 1904, 13 September 1905, 28 July and 17 October 1906, 11 February and 24 May 1916, and 5 September 1917 (quotations from 2 September 1882, box 1, and 23 May 1904, box 1).

57. T. J. Morgan, CIA, to All U.S. Indian Agents, 8 March 1890, Abbott to CIA, 30 June 1913, RCUA, 44014, folder "Fairs," box 1. Werner to CIA, 7 July 1911, RCUA, 44011.

58. *SANR*, 1911–22, RCUA, 44016, box 8; Farming and Grazing Leases, RCUA, 44097–98, Land, Farming and Grazing Leases, boxes 138–43; Mineral Leases, RCUA, 44099, Land, Mineral Leases, boxes 143–45; "Amended Rules and Regulations To Be Observed in the Execution of Leases of Indian Allotments," RCUA, 44017, folder "Land Regulations and Circulars, 1878–1942," box 11; Hall Report, Section C.; Fiske Report; Swadesh, "Southern Utes."

59. Werner to CIA, 28 February 1907; and Werner to F. H. Roberts, 1 June 1907, RCUA, 44011; West to Mr. W. Zabriska, 17 January 1916, RCUA, 44013.

60. Correspondence on women's financial dealings drawn from the bound letterbooks of 1905–17 is too plentiful to cite in detail. Fifty-five references are found in three boxes of letterbooks: 44011 contains twenty-nine, 44012 has sixteen, and 44013 has ten. Of these, thirty-four discuss land transactions.

61. Mary Baker Pena to CIA 9 November 1925, Selected Documents; Pettit, *Utes*, 147; Jorgensen, *Sun Dance*, 97–99. Land alienation was the primary result of land policy under the Dawes Act (see McDonnell, *Dispossession*).

CHAPTER 4

1. The field matrons program grew out of nineteenth-century Euro-American ideology of "true womanhood." For discussion of this philosophy, see Mary P. Ryan, *Womanhood in America*, 2d ed. (New York: New Viewpoints, 1974), 75; Linda K. Kerber, *Women of the Republic: Intellect and Ideology in Revolutionary America* (New York: W. W. Norton & Company, 1980), 265–88; Nancy F. Cott, *The Bonds of Womanhood: Woman's Sphere in New England, 1780–1835* (New Haven: Yale University Press, 1977), 2–7; Barbara Welter, "The Cult of True Womanhood: 1820–1860," *American Quarterly* 18, 4 (1966): 151–74; and Mary P. Ryan, *Cradle of the Middle Class: The Family in Oneida County New York, 1780–1865* (Cambridge, U.K.: Cambridge University Press, 1981), 145–86, 200–210. For an alternative model for proper female behavior in nineteenth-century America, see Frances B. Cogan, in *All-American Girl: The Ideal of Real Womanhood in Mid-Nineteenth-Century America* (Athens and London: University of Georgia Press, 1989).

2. E. M. Kingsley, Inspector for the Board of Indian Commissioner, *ARBIC*, 1878, 53; William F. Vilas, Secretary of the Interior, to the President Pro-Tempore of the Senate, 3 May 1888, 50th Cong., 1st sess., 1888, Senate Exec. Doc. 160, 1; Mrs. Merial Dorchester, Special Agent for the Indian School Service, in *ARCIA*, 1891, 542; J. C. D. Atkins, CIA, to Vilas, 18 April 1888, 50th Cong., 1st sess., 1888, Senate Exec. Doc. 160, 2; Morgan, "Field Matrons," *ARCIA*, 1892, 101–2; D. M. Browning, CIA, *ARCIA*, 1893, 56; Cato Sells, CIA, Circular No. 992, "To All Superintendents and Field Matrons, 29 May 1915," M1121, roll 10, RG 75, NARA, Wash-

ington, D.C.. Data for the field matrons is found in their personnel files, agents' annual reports, and in scattered letters by various OIA officials. Only a handful of their actual reports has survived in the OIA records.

3. For a more complete discussion of the Ute matrons see Katherine M. B. Osburn, " 'And as the Squaws Are a Secondary Consideration': Southern Ute Women Under Directed Culture Change, 1887–1934" (Ph.D. diss., University of Denver, 1993), chapter 5. RCUA, 44018, Administration and Control, Employees Files, folder "Louis Knackstead," box 17; Charles Werner, SUA, to CIA, 9 May 1908, RCUA, 44011; Personnel File of Nina McCaw, and Personnel File of Cecil Shields, RCUA, 44018, box 17; "Financial Report, Southern Ute Agency," 3 March 1910, RCUA, 44016, box 8; Personnel Files for the matrons in RCUA, 44018: Josephine Belt, Lena Boroughs, and Cora Abbot, box 14; Lizzie McCorquordale, Mellie Martin, Cora Hutchinson, Martha Morris, Nina McCaw, Minnie Knackstead, and Cecil Shields, box 17; RCUA, 44016, folder "Employee Changes, Regular, Irregular," box 12; Walter West, SAU, to CIA, 4 June 1917, RCUA, 44013.

4. Morgan, "Field Matrons," *ARCIA*, 1892, 100–101.

5. "Industrial Survey, 1929," RCUA, 44105, box 162.

6. Ibid.; Warren A. Ferris, *Life in the Rocky Mountains*, edited by Paul C. Phillips (Denver: The Old West Publishing Company, 1940), 278–79.

7. *ARCIA*, 1910, 23. For the importance of private property to "civilization," see Hoxie, *Final Promise*, 19–29.

8. The two people who lived alone were 32-year-old George Watts and 88-year-old widow Jane Storm. Of the extended families, twelve were female-headed: nine women living with their unmarried, widowed, or divorced children and grandchildren, one woman living with her two small children and her brother, one 53-year-old living with minor children whose relationship to her was unclear, and one woman living with a married couple, whose relationship to her was unclear. The remaining thirty-five extended-family households had twenty-three families containing a husband, wife, and relatives of either spouse, and twelve male-headed households that contained either no wife or a woman whose relationship to the man was unclear ("Industrial Survey, 1929," RCUA, 44105, box 162; Opler, "Southern Ute," 182).

9. "Industrial Survey, 1929," RCUA, 44105, box 162. For two of the houses no information on their condition is available.

10. Beginning in 1900, among men and women forty-six and older, nineteen women (out of thirty-six) and twenty-one men (out of thirty-two) had young children living at home; in 1912, thirteen women (out of thirty-eight) and eighteen men (out of thirty-seven) lived with small children; in 1923 the numbers were twenty-one women (out of forty-six) and twenty men (out of thirty-one); in 1932, eighteen women (out of thirty-eight) and sixteen men (out of thirty-two) had little children in their homes. In 1923 the fifty-six-plus group constituted 20 percent of all women living with children on the reservation (Census Summary, 1900, 1912, 1923, 1932, Southern Ute Census Records, Stewart Collection, Series II, box 4).

11. The idea that mothers were the primary civilizing force appears throughout the OIA records of the late nineteenth and early twentieth centuries (see note 2, this chapter, for specific references).

12. William D. Leonard, SUA, to CIA, 4 January 1907, RCUA, 44011; North File, RCUA, 44015, box 5; Sage File, RCUA, box 6; David A. Day, SUA, to CIA, 12 April 1904, RCUA, 44012; Bird File and Buck File, RCUA, box 4; Heirship Case of John Alden, 9 December 1907, RCUA, 44011; Burton B. Custer, SUA, to William Peterson, Navajo Springs, Colorado, 13 March 1905, RCUA, 44012; Brown File, RCUA, 44012, box 4; Chavez File and Cook File, RCUA, 44012, box 4; Leonard to CIA, 21 September 1906; Custer to CIA, 27 December 1905; and Walter Runke, SUA, to Claude Covey, Superintendent, Navajo Springs, 16 December 1913, RCUA, 44012; Custer to Peterson, 20 November 1905, RCUA, 44012; RCUA, 44015, box 4, Buck File; Edward E. McKean, SUA, to Gross, 1 and 7 October 1925, RCUA, box 5, Myore File; Cook File, RCUA, box 4; Abbot to CIA, 8 July 1913, RCUA, 44011; "Annuity payments to orphans, 1 January 1903," RCUA, 44012.

13. *ARCIA*, 1910, 5–8, M1011; "Special Report of R. E. L. Newburne, Inspector, 26 March to 2 April 1916," CCF-SU, 41803–700, 1 (hereafter cited as Newburne Report); Asbury Report; Michael Report; *ARCIA*, 1919, 5, M1011; McConihe Report, Health Section, 44–46; *ARCIA*, 1915, 4, RCUA, 44016.

14. *ARCIA*, 1910, 5; 1911, 5, M1011; Summary of mortality statistics for 1910–20, *SANR*, RCUA, 44016, box 8; Werner to CIA, 4 February 1911, CCF-SU, 16138; West to CIA, 28 April 1916, CCF-SU, 49082; Dr. Lee Curran, Agency Physician, to West, 17 May 1916, RCUA, 44013; McConihe Report, Health Section, 1, 44.

15. "Report of Dr. Paul Capps, Agency Physician, 17 October 1917," CCF-SU, 111436; Capps to CIA, telegram, 17 October 1914, CCF-SU, 111436; Newburne Report, 2; Newton Report, 1915, 150; McConihe Report, Health Section, 1, 42–44, 48; West to CIA, 27 September 1916, RCUA, 44013; "Quarterly Reports of Martha P. Morris for 1914," RCUA, 44016, box 8.

16. West to CIA, 16 May 1916, RCUA, 44013; *ARCIA*, 1916, unpaginated, M1011; Curran to West, 16 May 1916, RCUA, 44013.

17. Summary of Statistics on Income, 1911–22, RCUA, 44016, boxes 8–9. The "progressive" families may have farmed but still held to very "traditional" cultural practices. Nevertheless, it would be logical for Ute women whose husbands were prosperous farmers to be more amenable to the matrons' ideas than women married to less "successful" men. For a discussion of the problem of determining levels of acculturation, see David Rich Lewis, "Reservation Leadership and the Progressive-Traditional Dichotomy: William Wash and the Northern Utes, 1865–1928," *Ethnohistory* 38, 1 (1991): 124–42; West to CIA, 29 April 1916, CCF-SU, 49082.

18. West to CIA, 9 May 1917, RCUA, 44013.

19. West to CIA, 27 September 1916, RCUA, 44013; *ARCIA*, 1917, unpaginated, M1011; Michael Report, 3; Summary of Statistics on Infant Deaths, 1911–25, RCUA, 44016, boxes 8–9; *ARCIA*, 1922, unpaginated, M1011; "Report of

Horace G. Wilson, Supervisor, 1919," CCF-SU, 6370–700 (hereafter cited as Wilson Report); Wilson to McKean, 24 May 1919, CCF-SU, 92877–1541.

20. Summary of Statistics on Infant Deaths, RCUA, 44016, boxes 8–9.

21. Census Summary of 1880, 1900, 1912, 1923, 1932; Monthly Sanitary Reports, 1879–94, and Quarterly Sanitary Reports, 1895–1909, RCUA, 44103, boxes 155–56; *SANR*, 1911–18, RCUA, 44016, boxes 7–8.

22. McCorquordale attempted to save two Utes who had been left to die of exposure — a newborn twin infant and an elderly woman. Lizzie managed to save the woman but, despite her "constant attention for four days and nights," the baby died (Reports of Lizzie McCorquordale for April through November 1910, RCUA, 44016, box 8). Reports of Mellie Martin, May 1911, RCUA, 8; *ARCIA*, 1910, 8; 1911, 5; 1912, 5; "Quarterly Reports of Martha Morris for 1914," RCUA, 44016, box 8; Wilson Report, Testimony of Josephine Belt.

23. Catherine S. Fowler, "Subsistence," in d'Azevedo, *Great Basin*, 69; Opler, "Southern Ute," 139–40; Frank Blachly, Monthly Reports, September 1890, RCUA, 44103, box 156; and Carl Lefforge, Agency Physician, to Edward Peacore, 5 May 1930, CCF-CU, 735–28785.

24. For a discussion of how field nurses replaced matrons in New Mexico, see Sandra Schackel, *Social Housekeepers: Women Shaping Public Policy in New Mexico, 1920–1940* (Albuquerque: University of New Mexico Press, 1992), chapter 3. Werner to CIA, 28 January 1909, CCF-SU, 732; Abbot to CIA, 23 July 1913; West to CIA, 4 September 1914; West to CIA (quoting Capps), 27 August 1914; and Capps to CIA, 25 August 1914, RCUA, 44011; McConihe Report, Health Section, 42; Asbury Report, 9; John W. Atwater to CIA, 27–31 January 1922, CCF-CU, 710–10474; Reports of the field nurses, 1929–34, RCUA, box 156; Carl Lefforge, Agency Physician, to Edward Peacore, 5 May 1930, CCF-CU, 735–28785. The education office of the Southern Ute Tribe informed me that the hospital was built in 1931. Swadesh ("Southern Utes," 167–68), and Opler ("Southern Ute," 196–97) also note that after 1930 women at Southern Ute were more willing to have children in the hospital.

25. Morgan, "Field Matrons," *ARCIA*, 1892, 100–101.

26. Reports of Lizzie McCorquordale for April through November 1910, RCUA, 44016, box 8. The story of the dying infant is found in November's report. Summary of Lizzie McCorquordale Reports, RCUA, 44016, box 8. Reports of Mellie P. Martin for March, July, and October 1911, RCUA, 44016, box 8; Martin, Report for April 1911. Martin, Reports for May and July 1911; ARCIA, 1911, 5; 1912, M1011; Martin, Reports for March and October 1911. Summary of Reports of Martha Morris, 1914–17, RCUA, box 8. Wilson Report, Testimony of Josephine Belt.

27. Wilson Report; *ARCIA*, 1920, unpaginated, M1011; Michael Report, Health Section.

28. Opler, "Southern Ute," 131; Callaway, Janetski, and Stewart, "Ute," in d'Azevedo, *Great Basin*, 342–43. Anglos who settled near the Ute reservation at the turn

of the century recalled how Ute women frequently came to their homes to visit and borrow their sewing machines. See the interviews of Sarah Randall James and Rosa Belle Lines, Montrose County; Emma Daum Amick, Rio Blanco County; Jessie Omert, Chafee County; Mella McClover Bohlick, La Plata County; Mary and C. L. Goff, Christopher Columbus, James B. Lowe, Thomas Roberts, Delta County (WPA Interviews, 1933–34, Colorado Historical Society, Denver, Colorado).

29. Ibid.; Wilson Report.

30. Summary of Reports on Southern Ute Fairs, and Charles F. Werner, "First Annual Fair, Southern Ute Agency, 1907," and folder "Educational Exhibits, Southern Ute Fair, 1907–1935," RCUA, 44015, box 161; West to CIA, 15 May and 12 October 1916, RCUA, 44013.

31. Walter Runke, "Report on the 1914 Southern Ute Fair," RCUA, 44105, box 161.

32. "First Annual Fair, Southern Ute, Colorado," RCUA, 44105, box 161; Runke to CIA, 28 July 1914, RCUA, 44012; West to CIA, 12 October 1916, RCUA, 44013.

33. "First Annual Fair, Southern Ute, Colorado," RCUA, 44105, box 161; Callaway, Janetski, and Stewart, "Ute," in d'Azevedo, *Great Basin*, 343–51; Conn, *Persistent Vision*. Carol Satersmoen, "Cultural Change Among the Northern and Southern Utes as Represented by the Beadwork Collections of the Colorado Historical Society" (unpublished master's paper, Department of Anthropology Library, University of Denver, Denver, Colorado, 1990).

34. West to CIA, 15 May 1916, RCUA, 44013; Walter G. West, "Announcement of Adult Industrial Contest, May 12–17," RCUA, 44013.

35. Page to CIA, 2 June 1880, RCUA, 44010; Charles A. Bartholomew, SUA, to CIA, 18 June 1890, RCUA, 44010; Francis E. Leupp, "Southern Ute," 1002; Werner to CIA, 22 September 1910, RCUA, 44011.

36. *ARBIC*, 1878, 52–55; 1879, 8–12; *ARCIA*, 1891, 542–48; 1892, 100–102; 1900, 450–59; West to CIA, 18 April 1916, West to CIA, 27 September 1916, RCUA, 44013; *ARCIA*, 1918, 5–6, M1011; Edward E. McKean, "Industrial Surveys, 1922 and 1929," RCUA, 44005, Accounts, Ledgers, box 162. Evaluation of a "well-furnished house" must be accepted with some skepticism for eight of these homes were quite dilapidated.

37. "Report of G. E. E. Lindquist, 23 December 1931," Papers of General Hugh H. Scott, Member, Board of Indian Commissioners, RG 838-Ute, I-040, roll 2, Center for Southwest Studies, Fort Lewis College, Durango, Colorado (hereafter cited as Scott Papers); Charles E. Farin, Supervisor of Indian Industries, to CIA, 30 March 1929, CCF-CU, 20137; Rosemary Trant, Teacher of Home Economics, to Peacore, 24 August 1934, CCF-CU, 01–917.

38. "Industrial Survey, 1929," RCUA, 44005, box 162.

39. Mrs. Cora Dunn, "More Systematic Training Along Industrial Lines," Address at Charleston, South Carolina, Before the Department of Indian Education, in *ARCIA*, 1900, 190; *ARCIA*, 1904, 432.

CHAPTER 5

1. CIA to Mr. H. F. Roller, Examiner of Inheritance, Ft. Washakie, Wyoming, 2 July 1915, CCF-SU, 740–64051.

2. Schmeckebier, *Office of Indian Affairs*, 257–58; CIA to Edward McKean, SUA, 28 December 1917, CCF-SU, 104064; M. Smith, "History," 232–42; *Rulebook*, 4.

3. For an overview of American sexuality through history, see John D'Emilio and Estelle B. Freedman, *Intimate Matters: A History of Sexuality in America* (New York: Harper & Row, 1988). On women's "purity," see Nancy F. Cott "Passionlessness: An Interpretation of Victorian Sexual Ideology, 1790–1850," *Signs* 4 (1978): 219–36, and Daniel Scott Smith, "Family Limitation, Sexual Control and Domestic Feminism in Victorian America," *Feminist Studies* 1 (Winter–Spring 1973): 40–57. For a study that compares some women's actual sexual experiences to the prescriptive literature, see Carl Degler, "What Ought to Be and What Was: Women's Sexuality in the Nineteenth Century," *American Historical Review* 79 (1974): 479–90, and a critique of Degler's work, Carol Z. Stearns and Peter N. Stearns, "Victorian Sexuality: Can Historians Do It Better?" *Journal of Social History* 18 (1984–85): 626–33. Laura McCall's work questions whether the idea of women's "passionlessness" is an accurate paradigm for nineteenth-century sexual attitudes (see " 'With All the Wild, Trembling, Rapturous Feelings of a Lover': Men, Women, and Sexuality in American Literature, 1820–1860," *Journal of the Early Republic* 14 [Spring 1994]: 71–89). Morgan, "Field Matrons," *ARCIA*, 1892, 101; Mrs. Cora Dunn, Superintendent, Rainy Mountain School, Anadarko, Oklahoma, "More Systematic Training Along Industrial Lines," *ARCIA*, 1900, 452.

4. Racism also marked attitudes about the virtue of black or Hispanic women, who were often viewed as morally deficient. See Jacqueline Jones, *Labor of Love, Labor of Sorrow: Black Women, Work, and the Family from Slavery to the Present* (New York: Basic Books, Inc., 1985), 149–150, and Frederick B. Pike, *The United States and Latin America: Myths and Stereotypes of Civilization and Nature* (Austin: University of Texas Press, 1992), chapter 2.

5. *ARCIA*, 1877, 48; 1890, 23; 1913, RCUA, 44016, box 7. All narrative annual reports after 1910 are either found in boxes 7–8 of this series or in *SANR*, 1907–38, M1011, roll 143; *ARCIA*, 1893, 133; 1894, 127; William D. Leonard, SUA, to CIA, 10 July 1906, RCUA, 44011; *ARCIA*, 1907, RCUA, 44011.

6. Opler, "Southern Ute," 146–48.

7. Ibid., 149–52.

8. After the introduction of the horse, women's sexual freedom remained, but the warrior culture introduced a form of institutionalized rape. The Dog Company, a military training society, sometimes captured women whom they laughed at and held in their camp for sexual purposes (Opler, "Southern Ute," 146–52, 162–66).

9. School Physician of the Santa Fe Indian School (name illegible), to Frederick Snyder, Superintendent, Santa Fe School, 27 December 1912, RCUA, 44015, box 6, W. File (to protect the women's anonymity, all family files will be cited using

initials only); Snyder to Charles McChesney, SUA, 29 December 1912, RCUA, 44015, box 6, W. File.

10. McChesney to Snyder, 2 January 1913, RCUA, 44015, box 6, W. File; "1923 Census of the Southern Ute Tribe," Stewart Collection, and "1932 Census of the Southern Ute Tribe," Stewart Collection (hereafter cited as 1923 Census and 1932 Census).

11. G. E. Williams, Superintendent of Jicarilla Agency to Werner, 22 and 24 March 1910; and E. O. Greene, Superintendent, Jicarilla Agency, to Abbot, 25 March 1913, RCUA, 44015, box 4, B. File; Newton Report, 1915.

12. *SANR*, 1916–17, Employment Section, RCUA, 44016, box 7; West to CIA, 24 January 1917, RCUA, 44013; *ARCIA*, 1916, M1011; A. B. to McKean, 20 October 1917; and McKean to A. B., 26 December 1917, RCUA, 44015, B. File.

13. A. B. to McKean, 20 October 1917, RCUA, 44015, B. File.

14. A. B. to Edward McKean, October 1917; McKean to A. B., 26 December 1917; and Snyder to McKean, 7 March 1918, RCUA, 44015, B. File; 1912 Census, Stewart Collection.

15. Examiner of Inheritance, Jicarilla Agency, 17 June 1927, RCUA, 44015, B. File; Edward J. Peacore to C. L. Graves, Superintendent, Jicarilla Agency, 27 June 1930, RCUA, 44015, B. File. Jacob Box, Southern Ute Reservation, to J. D. Huff, Superintendent, Santa Fe Indian School, 7 February 1919, RCUA, 44015, Records of the Santa Fe Indian School, entry 47, box 1, B. Folder.

16. Newton Report, 1915; Joseph D. Turner, Superintendent, Allen day school, to Abbot, 3 April 1913, RCUA, 44015, box 6, T. File.

17. Ibid.

18. Clerk, Southern Ute Agency, to West, Pueblo, Colorado, 5 April 1916; and West to Snyder, 11 April 1916, RCUA, 44015, box 6, T. File.

19. 1923 Census and 1930 Census, Stewart Collection; Annual School Reports, 1926–32, RCUA, 44016, box 8; one of E. T.'s grandsons informed me that she had several children with different partners and that there was no shame involved in this for his grandmother (personal communication, 1994).

20. West to Snyder, 21 December 1916, Shoshone Student File.

21. McKean to CIA, 28 August 1918, CCF-SU, 820–72101; J. D. Huff, Superintendent, Santa Fe School, to CIA, 5 October 1918, CCF-SU, 820–72101; and CIA to F. M. Conser, Superintendent, The Sherman Institute, 17 October 1918, CCF-SU, 820–72101.

22. West to Snyder, 13 March 1917, Shoshone Student File.

23. "Full Age-Minors," and "Rape-Age-What Constitutes-Penalty," *Mills Annotated Statutes of the State of Colorado* (Revised Supplement), vol. 3 (Denver: The Mills Publishing Company: 1904), 1305, 345. Perusal of law books until 1935 found no evidence that these laws were ever overturned.

24. "What Marriages Prohibited-Color-Consanguinity," in *1935 Colorado Statues Annotated*, vol. 4 (Denver: The Bradford-Robinson Printing Company, 1935), 56–57; racist remarks by agents against Hispanics are too numerous to list, but a

systematic study of Ute-Hispanic relations may be found in Swadesh, "Southern Utes." For West's remarks, see *ARCIA*, 1915–17, 2–3, RCUA, 44016.

25. Leonard to CIA, 3 November 1906, RCUA, 44012.

26. Heirship Papers of John Alden, 9 December 1907, RCUA, 44011; Statute of 28 February 1891, quoted in Schmeckebier, *Office of Indian Affairs*, 444.

27. They were probably tried before the Court of Indian Offenses. *ARCIA*, 1911, RCUA, 44016; 1912, M1011; Marriage Records, SUA Letters.

28. Werner to CIA, 2 June 1911, CCF-SU, 53094.

29. The last name of this family has been changed to protect privacy. Since Utes sometimes gave their children up for adoption of their own volition it is possible that Werner did not have to coerce the Browns into giving up Mary. Werner to CIA, 11 November 1910, RCUA, 44011; Data on the Brown family taken from 1912 Census, Stewart Collection.

30. Werner to CIA, 3 January 1911, RCUA, 44011; Werner to CIA, 6 August 1912, CCF-SU, 722.1–9047–1910; CIA to Werner, 20 August 1912; and Mc-Chesney to CIA, 7 October 1912, CCF-SU, 722.1–90847–1910; H. R. Hummer, Superintendent, Canton Asylum for Insane Indians, to McChesney, 4 October 1912, RCUA, 44015, box 4, Brown File.

31. Hummer to CIA, 12 October 1912, CCF-SU, 722.1–90847–1910; Hummer to McChesney, 10 March 1913, RCUA, 44015, box 4, Brown File.

32. Abbot to CIA, 9 May 1913, RCUA, 44015, box 4, Brown File; Stephen Abbot, SAU, to CIA, 19 June 1913, RCUA, 44011; Abbot to CIA, 10 July 1913, RCUA, 44012.

33. Hummer to CIA, 9 September 1913 and 1 February 1916, CCF-SU, 722.1–90847–1910. Following Jane's death, her father anxiously requested Agent McKean have his son Sam returned from the Santa Fe Indian School (see McKean to Frederick Snyder, Santa Fe, RCUA, 44015, box 4, Brown File.

34. Walter Runke, SUA, to Hummer, 8 December 1913, RCUA, 44011; Werner to CIA, 6 August 1912, CCF-SU, 722.1–90847–1910; Abbot to CIA, 9 May 1913, RCUA, 44015, box 4, Brown File; Abbot to CIA, 3 September 1913, RCUA, 44011. The agents' behavior concerning women who were judged to be mentally incompetent mirrored the larger eugenics movement of the late nineteenth and early twentieth centuries (see Philip Reilly, *The Surgical Solution: A History of Involuntary Sterilization in the United States* [Baltimore: Johns Hopkins University Press, 1991]), and Edward J. Larson, *Sex, Race, and Science: Eugenics in the Deep South* (Baltimore: John Hopkins University Press, 1995).

35. Werner to CIA, 27 July 1911, RCUA, 44015, box 5, M. File.

36. OIA records do not indicate exactly what procedure Werner used to annul K.M.'s marriage. Jim P. may have decided he didn't want K. M. (or vice versa), and Werner may have overstated his role in the conflict. Werner to Uintah-Ouray, 14 August 1911; Werner to CIA, 27 July 1911; Werner to Uintah-Ouray, 20 May 1912; McChesney to Captain Brees, Uintah-Ouray, 4 June 1913; Walter G. West, SUA, to Albert K. Kneale, Superintendent, Uintah-Ouray; F. A. Gross, Clerk, Uintah-

Ouray, to Southern Ute Agent, 6 and 20 September 1917; West to Kneale, 16 November 1917; and Gross to McKean, 19 May 1924, RCUA, 44015, box 5, M. File.

37. Opler, "Southern Ute," 152; *ARCIA*, 1894, 127.

38. U. L. Gready, Navajo Springs Agent (NSA), to Werner, 3 July 1910, RCUA, 44015, box 5, N. File; 1912 Census, Stewart Collection.

39. Oral Histories, FLC. McKean to C. J. Crandall, Superintendent, Northern Pueblo, Santa Fe, New Mexico, 28 February 1924; and McKean to Crandall, and McKean to CIA, 28 February 1924, CCF-CU, 743–17186.

40. E. B. Meritt, Assistant CIA, to McKean, 20 May 1924, CCF-CU, 743–17186.

41. 1930 Census.

42. Oral Histories, FLC; *The Ignacio Chieftain*, obituary for John Taylor, 10 January 1934, Helen Sloan Daniels Collection, RG 7, box 1, Center for Southwest Studies, Fort Lewis College, Durango, Colorado.

43. Leonard to Superintendent, Fort Lewis, 11 September 1906, RCUA, 44012; 1912 Census and 1923 Census, Stewart Collection; Death Records, Stewart Collection.

44. Roy Williams to "My dear Friend," CIA, 17 January 1930; and Peacore to CIA, 8 February 1930, CCF-CU, 740–3911.

45. *Rulebook*, 8.

46. West to CIA, 9 March 1917, RCUA, 44013. *Rulebook*, 8.

47. Twelve illegal and two legal divorces occurred at the same time. Since no names were recorded, it is impossible to know how they intersect with the marriages (*ARCIA*, 1913–18, M1011; Southern Ute Marriage Records, 1901–11, Stewart Collection (hereafter cited as Marriage Records); *SANR*, RCUA, 44016, boxes 7–8).

48. Marriage Records; *ARCIA*, 1911–25, Statistical Reports.

49. "G. E. E. Lindquist Report on the Southern Ute Reservation, November 1931," Scott Papers; Opler, "Southern Ute," 184–85, 196–98; Stewart's observation is found in Callaway, Janetski, and Stewart, "Ute," in d'Azevedo, *Great Basin*, 352.

50. See *ARCIA*, 1893–94, 1906–7, and *Rulebook*, 8, for assessments of the stability of tribal marriages. BLM Allotment Tract Book, at the BLM offices, Denver Federal Center; Southern Ute Death Records, Tri-Ethnic Files; Stewart Personal Papers; Runke to Tucker, Durango, Colorado, 6 January 1914, RCUA, 44012; *ARCIA*, 1890, 23.

51. Judith Shapiro, "Kinship," in d'Azevedo, *Great Basin*, 622–24; Callaway, Janetski, and Stewart, "Ute," in d'Azevedo, *Great Basin*, 352–53; Pettit, *Utes*, 60.

52. Historians studying the causes of divorce among Americans have noted a lengthy list of factors straining the institution of marriage. If the pressures of industrialization and urbanization caused major changes in Euro-American families how much more would a deliberate assault on every aspect of native cultures strain Indian families? See Glenda Riley, *Divorce: An American Tradition* (New York: Oxford University Press, 1991), 5.

53. Monthly Sanitary Reports, July 1882, RCUA, 44103, box 162; *ARCIA*, 1882, 18; Monthly Sanitary Reports, April 1884, RCUA, 44103, box 162; *ARCIA*, 1884, 18–20.

54. Henry Page, SUA, to CIA, 29 May 1879, LROIA-CS, M234, roll 211, 1879.

55. While not dealing specifically with women from the Southern bands, this incident reveals Ute women's vulnerability. George Burnett, 1st Lieut., 9th U.S. Cavalry, to Adjutant General, Department of the Platte, Omaha, Nebraska, 10 September 1887, LROIA, 1887: 26594.

56. Werner to CIA, 21 March 1909; and A. W. Robbins, M.D., to Werner, 11 March 1909, CCF-SU, 734–20514–09.

57. Werner to CIA, 21 March 1909; Robbins to Werner, 11 March 1909; and Werner to CIA, 21 March 1909, CCF-SU, 734–20514–09.

58. *The People v. Black Rock*, La Plata County Court No. 796, filed, 8 April 1910, docket no. 68726 in the State Archives of Colorado; 1900 Census and 1912; Werner to CIA, 23 May 1911, RCUA, 44011; Werner to Charles Pike, District Judge, Durango, Colorado, 28 August 1911; and Werner to CIA, 11 September 1911, RCUA, 44014, folder "Jurisdiction of Indian Courts," box 2; Pictures accompanying *ARCIA*, 1920, M1011.

59. Schmeckebier, *Office of Indian Affairs*, 256; Hoxie, *Final Promise*, 225–30.

60. Hoxie, *Final Promise*, 225–30; *U.S. Statutes at Large* 35 (1909), 1151.

61. The next mention of rape was a passing remark in the "Law and Order" section of the 1921 annual report. Agent McKean reported that a 25-year-old Indian woman claimed to have been raped by two white men; no details are available (*SANR*, 1921, Law and Order Section, RCUA, 44016, box 8, 3).

62. Antonio Buck to CIA, 24 April 1929, CCF-CU, 175–22111; Charles H. Burke, CIA, to Antonio Buck, Jr., Ignacio, Colorado, 7 May 1929; and Burke to Edward H. Peacore, SUA, 7 May 1929, CCF-CU, 175–22111.

63. Peacore to CIA, 14 May 1929, CCF-CU, 175–22111.

64. Statement of Sheriff Ed Painter, Durango, Colorado, 17 September 1929; Statement of Charles Adams, 15 September 1929; and Statement of V. A., 16 September 1929, "Investigation of H. J. Stricken, 15–17 September 1929," CCF-CU, 48123.

65. Ibid.

66. Mrs. C. W. Wiegel to Charles S. Rhodes, CIA, 24 November 1931, CCF-CU, 154–55399, Nash-Hagerman Report, pt. 1.

67. Peacore to Mr. A. L. Kroeger, member, Colorado State Indian Commission, Durango, Colorado, 12 January 1932, Nash-Hagerman Report, pt. 1.

68. Wiegel to CIA, 24 November 1931, Peacore to CIA, 17 November 1931; and Lottie McCall, Red Lake, Minnesota, to Wiegel, 28 October 1931, Nash-Hagerman Report, pt. 1.

69. Peacore to CIA, 17 November 1931, Nash-Hagerman Report, pt. 1.

70. "Affidavit of S. D. H.," Nash-Hagerman Report, pt. 1.

71. McCall to Wiegel, 28 October 1931, Nash-Hagerman Report, pt. 1.

72. Peacore to CIA, 12 January 1932, Nash-Hagerman Report, pt. 1.

73. A. L. Kroeger, Colorado State Indian Commission, to Governor William Adams, 15 February 1932, Nash-Hagerman Report, pt. 3.

74. Roy Nash to CIA, 19 October 1931, Nash-Hagerman Report, pt. 1.

75. Charles A. Bartholomew to CIA, 25 April 1891, RCUA, 44010.

76. Ibid.

77. Nash to CIA, 19 October 1931, Nash-Hagerman Report, pt. 1. Mr. Peacore and his wife were Chipewa. See Memo from H. J. Hagerman, 18 January 1932, Nash-Hagerman Report, pt. 1.

78. Rayna Green, "The Pocahontas Perplex: The Image of Indian Women in American Culture," *Massachusetts Review* 16, 4 (1975): 698–714; David Smits, "The 'Squaw Drudge': A Prime Index of Savagism," *Ethnohistory* 29, 4 (1982): 281–306; Kidwell, "Indian Women," 97–107. For remarks on the sexuality of African-American or Hispanic women, see Jones, *Labor of Love*, 149–50, and Pike, *Myths and Stereotypes*, chapter 2.

79. Because the historical record is fragmentary, it is impossible to know whether these women were forced to submit to the agent's authority later in their lives or if they suffered any consequences for their rebellion.

CONCLUSION

1. Weaver to CIA, 15 December 1877, RCUA, 44010.

2. Ute women expressed this view of their roles in oral histories collected in *Colorado Women's History: A Multicultural Treasury*, edited by Sue Ann Schnellman (Denver: The Colorado Commission for Women's History, 1985). The Utes still honor elder women and consider grandmothers especially important for child rearing. The Bear Dance, celebrating women's fertility, is still a special annual event on the reservation. Other Indian women offer a similar understanding of their roles in M. Annette Jaimes and Theresa Halsey, "American Indian Women," 311–44. Ute women who granted interviews for the Oral History Project at the Center for Southwest Studies, Durango, Colorado, stressed the importance of their role as keepers of tradition.

3. Hughes, *American Indians in Colorado*, 98–101; Callaway, Janetski, and Stewart, "Ute," in d'Azevedo, *Great Basin*, 361–63.

4. "Minutes of the Southern Ute Tribal Council, 1939–49," CCF-CU, 054–62027–1929, indicate that nine women served on the council both as members and as tribal clerks; Hughes, *American Indians in Colorado*, 98–101; Pettit, *Utes*, 152–57.

5. "Report of G. E. E. Lindquist, 23 December 1931," Scott Papers.

6. For background on women's changing public roles in the 1920s, see Daniel J. Walkowitz, "The Making of a Feminine Professional Identity: Social Workers in the 1920s," *American Historical Review* 95 (October 1980): 1051–75; and essays in Noralee Frankel and Nancy S. Dye, eds. *Gender, Class, Race, and Reform in the Progressive Era* (Lexington: University of Kentucky Press, 1991).

7. The Indian Reorganization Act, or "Indian New Deal," advocated a model of tribal government based on representative democracy. This ran counter to Native Americans' traditions of kinship-based government. Also, there is some debate as to whether or not the government coerced tribes into voting for this program. For a discussion of the transformation of Indian policy, see Frederick E. Hoxie, "The Curious Story of Reformers and the American Indian," in *Indians in American History* (Arlington Heights, Ill.: Harlan Davidson, Inc., 1988): 205–29, and Lawrence C. Kelly, *The Assault on Assimilation: John Collier and the Origins of Indian Policy Reform* (Albuquerque: University of New Mexico Press, 1981).

8. Anderson, *Chain Her By One Foot*; essays in Etienne and Leacock *Women and Colonization*; Alan M. Klein, "The Political-Economy of Gender: A 19th Century Plains Indian Case Study," in *The Hidden Half: Plains Indian Women*, edited by Patricia Albers and Beatrice Medicine (Lanham: University Press of America, 1983), 143–73; Margot Liberty, "Hell Came with Horses: Plains Indian Women in the Equestrian Era," *Montana* 32 (Fall 1982): 10–19; Theda Perdue, "Cherokee Women and the Trail of Tears," *Journal of Women's History* 1, 1 (1989): 14–30. For an insightful critique of the "declensionist" model, see Nancy Shoemaker, "The Rise or Fall of Iroquois Women," *Journal of Women's History* 2 (1991): 39–57.

9. The essays in *Women and Power*, edited by Klein and Ackerman, contain examples of each of these processes among Indian women. For economic decline, see Martha C. Knack, "The Dynamics of Southern Paiute Women's Roles," and Sue-Ellen Jacobs, "Continuity and Change in Gender Roles at San Juan Pueblo." For women's loss of political power, see Victoria Patterson, "Evolving Gender Roles in Pomo Society," and Henry S. Sharp, "Women and Men Among the Chipewyan." Knack and Jacobs also delineate the replacement of ideologies of complementary gender roles with hierarchical ones, yet each of the essays notes the ambiguity and complexity of gender relations, and other essays do not document a decline in women's relative positions within their society after contact (see especially, Lillian Ackerman, "Complementary But Equal: Gender Status in the Plateau").

10. Marla Powers, in *Oglala Women: Myth, Ritual, and Reality* (Chicago: University of Chicago Press, 1986), argues that because women's homemaking roles in the post-reservation period were a continuation of their pre-reservation responsibilities, their adjustment to the reservation was smoother than men's. A comparison of how Two Leggings and Pretty Shield, a Crow man and woman, adjust to reservation life reiterates this point. Frank Linderman, *Pretty Shield: A Crow Medicine Woman* (Lincoln: University of Nebraska Press, 1974); Peter Nabokov, *Two Leggings: The Making of a Crow Warrior* (Lincoln: University of Nebraska Press, 1967). Also see Clara Sue Kidwell, "The Power of Women in Three American Indian Societies," *Journal of Ethnic Studies* 6 (Fall 1978): 164–83. The literature documenting how native peoples both accommodate to and resist colonialism is too voluminous to cite, but a good introduction to the topic is Spicer, "Types of Contact."

Selected Bibliography

MANUSCRIPT COLLECTIONS

Center for Southwest Studies, Fort Lewis College, Durango, Colorado.
Microfilm Collection, I-053, roll 1. Southern Ute Agency Letters. Board of Indian
     Commissioners, 1919–33.
Record Group 7. Helen Sloan Daniels Collection.
Record Group 838-Ute, I-040, roll 2. Papers of General Hugh H. Scott.
Records of the Santa Fe Indian School.
"Selected Documents Relating to the Ute Indians, 1881–1939." Photocopy.
Colorado Historical Society, Denver, Colorado.
WPA Interviews, 1933–34.
Colorado State Federation of Women's Clubs Offices, Denver, Colorado.
The Colorado Clubwoman, 1925–32.
Convention Programs, 1895–1935.
Minutes of the Executive Board, 1914–22.
Yearbook Files, 1898–1934.
Norlin Library, University of Colorado, Boulder, Colorado. Western History Col-
     lections.
Omer Stewart Collection.
Omer Stewart's Personal Papers.
Papers of the Women's Christian Temperance Union of Colorado.
Tri-Ethnic Files.
The Presbyterian Historical Society, Philadelphia, Pennsylvania.
Biographical Folders of Missionaries.
The Home Mission Monthly, 1900–20.
Record Group 305.
Record Group 305.1.

Selected Bibliography

GOVERNMENT DOCUMENTS

Annual Report of the Commissioner of Indian Affairs. Washington, D.C.: Government Printing Office. Serial Sets.

Congress. House. Board of Indian Commissioners. "The Southern Ute," by Francis E. Leupp. In *Annual Report of the Board of Indian Commissioners*. 54th Cong., 1st sess., 1895. Serial 3382, 1001–2.

Congress. House. *The Southern Ute Indians of Colorado*. 52d Cong., 1st sess., 1892. Vol. 4. H. Rept. 1205. Serial 3043.

Congress. Senate. Committee on Indian Affairs. *Survey of Conditions of the Indians in the United States*. Pt. 19. Washington; D.C.: Government Printing Office, 1931, 10, 609–10, 704. Microfilm.

General Statutes, State of Colorado. Denver: Colorado Times Stream Printing and Publishing House, 1884, 1892.

U.S. Statutes at Large 35 (1909): 1151.

Regulations of the Indian Department. Washington, D.C.: Government Printing Office, 1884.

National Archives and Records Administration, Denver, Colorado. RG 75, Records of the Bureau of Indian Affairs.

Letters Received by the Office of Indian Affairs, The Colorado Superintendency. Microcopy 234, roll 211.

Records of the Consolidated Ute Agency, 1887–1952.

Reports of Inspections of the Field Jurisdictions of the Office of Indian Affairs, 1873–1900, Southern District. Microcopy 1070, roll 51.

National Archives and Records Administration, Washington, D.C. RG 75, Records of the Bureau of Indian Affairs.

Central Classified Files, Consolidated Ute Agency, 1922–34.

Central Classified Files, Southern Ute Agency, 1907–22.

Howard Wheeler, Act Files, 1011, A894, 1934.

Letters Received by the Office of Indian Affairs, 1881–1907.

Letters Sent by the Office of Indian Affairs, 1881–1907.

Records of the U.S. Senate. Special File 224, SEN83A-F9, box 50, no. 10 (RG 46). Special Cases 143.

PUBLISHED PRIMARY SOURCES

1935 Colorado Statues Annotated. Vol. 4. Denver: The Bradford-Robinson Printing Company, 1935.

Arthur, T. S. *Ten Nights in a Bar-room and What I Saw There*. Chicago: M. A. Donohue & Co., n.d.

Bain, Mrs. Edward. *History and Chronology of the Colorado State Federation of Women's Clubs, 1895–1955*. Denver: CSFWC, 1956.

Bradford, Mary C. *History and Chronology of the Colorado State Federation of Women's Clubs: 1895–1931*. Denver: CSFWC, 1932.

Brain, Belle M. *The Redemption of the Red Man*. New York: Board of Home Missions of the Presbyterian Church in the U.S.A., 1904.

Ferris, Warren A. *Life in the Rocky Mountains*. Edited by Paul C. Phillips. Denver: The Old West Publishing Company, 1940.

General Federation of Women's Clubs. *Sixty Years of Achievement, 1890–1950*. New York: GFWC, 1950.

Mills Annotated Statutes of the State of Colorado. Rev. Supplement. Vol. 3. Denver: The Mills Publishing Company, 1904.

Painter, C. C. *Removal of the Southern Utes*. Philadelphia: Indian Rights Association, 1890.

Powell, John Wesley. *Anthropology of the Numu: John Wesley Powell's Manuscripts on the Numu Peoples of Western North America, 1868–1880*. Edited by Don D. Fowler and Catherine S. Fowler. Smithsonian Contributions to Anthropology No. 14. Washington, D.C.: Smithsonian Institution, 1971.

———. "Sketch of the Mythology of the North American Indians." In *First Annual Report of the Bureau of American Ethnology for the Years 1879–1880*. Washington, D.C.: Government Printing Office, 1881.

Presbyterian Church of Colorado. *Historical Sketch of the Presbytery of Colorado*. Pueblo, Colo.: Privately Published, 1906.

Reed, Werner Z. *Lo-To-Kah*. Illustrated by Charles Craig and L. Maynard Dixon. New York: Continental Books, 1881.

BOOKS

Anderson, Karen. *Chain Her By One Foot: The Subjugation of Women in Seventeenth-Century New France*. New York: Routledge Press, 1991.

d'Azevedo, Warren L., et al., eds. *The Current Status of Anthropological Research in the Great Basin*. Reno: Desert Research Institute, 1966.

Bannan, Helen M. "True Womanhood on the Reservation: Field Matrons and the United States Indian Service." Working Paper No. 18. Albuquerque: Southwest Institute for Research on Women, 1984.

Barber, Ruth K., and Edith J. Agnew. *Sowers Went Forth: The Story of Presbyterian Missions in North New Mexico and Southern Colorado*. Albuquerque: Menaul Historical Library of the Southwest, 1981.

Bataille, Gretchen M., and Kathleen M. Sands. *American Indian Women: A Guide to Research*. New York: Garland Publishing, 1991.

———. *American Indian Women: Telling Their Lives*. Lincoln: University of Nebraska Press, 1984.

Berthrong, Donald J. *The Cheyenne and Arapaho Ordeal: Reservation and Agency Life in the Indian Territory, 1875–1907*. Norman: University of Oklahoma Press, 1976.

Blair, Karen. *The Clubwoman as Feminist: True Womanhood Redefined, 1862–1914.* New York: Holmes & Meier Publishing, Inc., 1980.

Borden, Ruth. *Frances Willard: A Biography.* Chapel Hill: University of North Carolina Press, 1986.

Brown, Jennifer S. H. *Strangers in Blood: Fur Trade Families in Indian Country.* Vancouver, Canada, and London: University of British Columbia Press, 1981.

Cline, Gloria Griffen. *Exploring the Great Basin.* Westport, Conn.: Greenwood Press, Publishers, 1963.

Conn, Richard. *A Persistent Vision: Art of the Reservation Days.* Seattle: University of Washington Press, for Denver Art Museum, 1986.

Cott, Nancy F. *The Bonds of Womanhood: "Women's Sphere" in New England, 1780–1835.* New Haven: Yale University Press, 1977.

Daniels, Helen Sloan, ed. *The Ute Indians in Southwestern Colorado.* Durango, Colo.: Durango Public Library Museum Project, 1941.

Delaney, Robert W. *The Ute Mountain Utes.* Albuquerque: University of New Mexico Press, 1989.

Deutsch, Sarah. *No Separate Refuge: Culture, Class, and Gender on an Anglo-Hispanic Frontier in the American Southwest 1880–1940.* New York: Oxford University Press, 1987.

Devens, Carol. *Countering Colonization: Native Women and Great Lakes Missions.* Berkeley: University of California Press, 1992.

Dippie, Brian W. *The Vanishing American: White Attitudes and U.S. Indian Policy.* Middletown, Conn.: Wesleyan University Press, 1982.

D'Emilio, John, and Estelle B. Freedman. *Intimate Matters: A History of Sexuality in America.* New York: Harper & Row, 1988.

Emmitt, Robert. *The Last War Trail: The Utes and the Settlement of Colorado.* Norman: University of Oklahoma Press, 1954.

Epstein, Barbara Leslie. *The Politics of Domesticity.* Middletown, Conn.: Wesleyan University Press, 1981.

Etienne, Mona, and Eleanor Leacock, eds. *Women and Colonization: An Anthropological Perspective.* New York: Praeger Publishing Inc., 1979.

Foster, Morris W. *Being Comanche: A Social History of an Indian Community.* Tucson: University of Arizona Press, 1991.

Frankel, Noralee, and Nancy S. Dye, eds. *Gender, Class, Race, and Reform in the Progressive Era.* Lexington: University of Kentucky Press, 1991.

Gordon, Linda. *Heroes of Their Own Lives: The Politics and History of Family Violence, Boston, 1880–1960.* New York: Viking Penguin Books, 1988.

———. *Woman's Body, Woman's Right.* New York: Penguin Books, 1976.

Gravel, Pierre B. "Nativity, Mobility and Household Size in a Tri-Ethnic Community." Research Report No. 46. Tri-Ethnic Research Project. Boulder: University of Colorado, 1963.

Green, Rayna. *Native American Women: A Contextual Bibliography.* Bloomington: Indiana University Press, 1983.

Hagan, William T. *The Indian Rights Association.* Tucson: The University of Arizona Press, 1985.

——. *United States–Comanche Relations: The Reservation Years.* New ed. Norman: University of Oklahoma Press, 1990.

Hartman, Mary S., and Lois Banner. *Class Consciousness Raised: New Perspectives on the History of Women.* New York: Harper & Row Publishers, 1974.

Herskovits, Melville J. *Acculturation.* Gloucester, Mass.: Peter Smith, 1958.

Horseman, Reginald. *Expansion and American Indian Policy, 1783–1812.* Detroit: Michigan State University Press, 1967.

Hoxie, Frederick E. *A Final Promise: The Campaign to Assimilate the Indians, 1880–1920.* Lincoln: University of Nebraska Press, 1984.

Hughes, J. Donald. *American Indians in Colorado.* 2d ed. Boulder: Pruett Publishing Company, 1987.

Hurt, Douglas R. *Indian Agriculture in America: Prehistory to the Present.* Lawrence: University Press of Kansas, 1987.

Hyer, Sally. *One House, One Voice, One Heart: Native American Education at the Santa Fe Indian School.* Santa Fe: Museum of New Mexico Press, 1990.

Jaimes, Annette M., ed. *The State of Native America.* Boston: South End Press, 1992.

Jefferson, James, Robert W. Delaney, and Gregory C. Thompson. *The Southern Ute: A Tribal History.* Ignacio, Colo.: The Southern Ute Tribe, 1972.

Jones, Jacqueline. *Labor of Love, Labor of Sorrow: Black Women, Work, and the Family from Slavery to the Present.* New York: Basic Books, Inc., 1985,

Jorgensen, Joseph G. *Sun Dance Religion.* Chicago: University of Chicago Press, 1972.

Kappler, Charles J. *Indian Affairs: Laws and Treaties.* Vols. 1–3. Washington, D.C.: Government Printing Office, 1904.

Keller, Robert H. *American Protestantism and United States Indian Policy, 1869–1882.* Lincoln: University of Nebraska Press, 1983.

Kelly, Lawrence C. *The Assault on Assimilation: John Collier and the Origins of Indian Policy Reform.* Albuquerque: University of New Mexico Press, 1981.

Kerber, Linda K. *Women of the Republic: Intellect and Ideology in Revolutionary America.* New York: W. W. Norton & Company, 1980.

Klein, Laura F., and Lillian A. Ackerman, eds. *Women and Power in Native North America.* Norman: University of Oklahoma Press, 1995.

Kvasnicka, Robert M., and Herman J. Viola, eds. *The Commissioners of Indian Affairs 1824–1977.* Lincoln: University of Nebraska Press, 1979.

Lewis, David Rich. *Neither Wolf nor Dog: American Indians, Environment and Agrarian Change.* New York: Oxford University Press, 1994.

Linderman, Frank. *Pretty Shield: A Crow Medicine Woman.* Lincoln: University of Nebraska Press, 1974.

Lomawaima, Tsianina, K. *They Called it Prairie Light: The Story of the Chilocco Indian School.* Lincoln: University of Nebraska Press, 1993.

Mark, Joan. *A Stranger in Her Native Land: Alice Fletcher and the American Indians.*
    Lincoln: University of Nebraska Press, 1988.
McDonnell, Janet A. *The Dispossession of the American Indian, 1887–1934.*
    Bloomington: Indiana University Press, 1991.
Mihesuah, Devon. *Cultivating the Rosebuds: The Education of Women at the Cherokee
    Female Seminary, 1851–1909.* Urbana: University of Illinois Press, 1993.
Nabokov, Peter. *Two Leggings: The Making of a Crow Warrior.* Lincoln: University
    of Nebraska Press, 1967.
Pascoe, Peggy. *Relations of Rescue: The Search for Female Moral Authority in the
    American West, 1874–1939.* New York: Oxford University Press, 1990.
Perry, Richard J. *Western Apache Heritage: People of the Mountain Corridor.* Austin:
    University of Texas Press, 1991.
Pettit, Jan. *Utes: The Mountain People.* Rev. ed. Boulder: Johnson Books, 1990.
Pike, Frederick B. *The United States and Latin America: Myths and Stereotypes of
    Civilization and Nature.* Austin: University of Texas Press, 1992.
Prucha, Francis P. *American Indian Policy in Crisis: Christian Reformers and the
    Indian, 1865–1900.* Norman: University of Oklahoma Press, 1976.
———. *The Churches and the Indian Schools, 1888–1912.* Lincoln: University of
    Nebraska Press, 1979.
Riley, Glenda. *Divorce: An American Tradition.* New York: Oxford University Press,
    1991.
Ruiz, Vicki L., and Ellen Carol DuBois, eds. *Unequal Sisters: A Multicultural Reader
    in U.S. Women's History.* 2d ed. New York: Routledge, 1994.
Ryan, Mary P. *Cradle of the Middle Class: The Family in Oneida County New York,
    1790–1865.* Cambridge, U.K.: Cambridge University Press, 1981.
———. *Womanhood in America.* 2d ed. New York: New Viewpoints, 1974.
Sanday, Peggy R. *Female Power and Male Dominance: On the Origins of Sexual
    Inequality.* Cambridge, U.K.: Cambridge University Press, 1981.
Schackel, Sandra. *Social Housekeepers: Women Shaping Public Policy in New Mexico,
    1920–1940.* Albuquerque: University of New Mexico Press, 1992.
Schlegel, Alice. *Male Dominance and Female Autonomy: Domestic Authority in
    Matrilineal Societies.* New Haven: Human Relations Area Files Press, 1972.
Shoemaker, Nancy, ed. *Negotiators of Change: Historical Perspectives on Native
    American Women.* New York: Routledge, 1995.
Smith, Anne. *Ute Tales.* Salt Lake City: University of Utah Press, 1992.
Smith, P. David. *Ouray, Chief of the Utes.* Ouray, Colo.: Wayfinders Press, 1986.
Spindler, Louise. *Menomini Women and Culture Change.* American Anthropological
    Association Memoir No. 91. N.p.: American Anthropological Association,
    1962.
Sprague, Marshall. *Massacre: The Tragedy of White River.* Lincoln: University of
    Nebraska Press, 1980.
Steward, Julian. *Basin-Plateau Aboriginal Sociopolitical Groups.* Salt Lake City:

University of Utah Press, 1970. Reprint of original Bureau of American
Ethnology Bulletin 120.

———. "Native Cultures of the Intermontane (Great Basin) Area." *Smithsonian
Miscellaneous Collections.* Vol. 100. Washington, D.C.: Smithsonian Institution,
1940.

———. *Theory of Culture Change.* Urbana, Ill.: University of Illinois Press, 1955.

Stewart, Omer C. *Ute Peyotism: A Study of a Cultural Complex.* University of
Colorado Series in Anthropology No. 1. Boulder: University of Colorado,
1948.

Stuart, Paul. *The Indian Office: Growth and Development of an American Institution,
1865–1900.* Ann Arbor: University Microfilms International, 1978.

Svaldi, David. *Sand Creek and the Rhetoric of Extermination.* New York: University
Press of America, 1989.

Swadesh, Frances Leon. *Los Primeros Pobladores: Hispanic Americans of the Ute
Frontier.* South Bend, Ind.: University of Notre Dame Press, 1974.

Szasz, Margaret, C. *Education and the American Indian.* Albuquerque: University of
New Mexico Press, 1974.

Thompson, Gregory Coyne. *Southern Ute Lands, 1848–1899: The Creation of a
Reservation.* Occasional Papers of the Center for Southwest Studies No. 1.
Durango, Colo.: Fort Lewis College, March 1972.

Ubbelohde, Carl, Maxine Benson, and Duane A. Smith. *A Colorado History.* 6th ed.
Boulder: Pruett Publishing Company, 1988.

Utley, Robert M. *The Indian Frontier of the American West, 1846–1890.*
Albuquerque: University of New Mexico Press, 1984.

Van Kirk, Sylvia. *Many Tender Ties: Women in Fur Trade Society, 1670–1870.*
Norman: University of Oklahoma Press, 1983.

White, Richard. *The Middle Ground: Indians, Empires, and Republics in the Great
Lakes Region, 1650–1815.* Cambridge, U.K.: Cambridge University Press,
1991.

Wilson, Rockwell. *The Utes, A Forgotten People.* Denver: Sage Books, 1956.

ARTICLES

Albers, Patricia, and William James. "Illusion and Illumination: Visual Images of
American Indian Women in the West." In *The Women's West,* edited by Susan
Armitage and Elizabeth Jameson. Norman: University of Oklahoma Press,
1987.

Banner, Lois W. "Religious Benevolence as Social Control: A Critique of an 'Interpretation.'" *Journal of American History* 50 (June 1973): 23–41.

Bell, Amelia Rector. "Separate People: Speaking of Cree Men and Women." *American Anthropologist* 92, 2 (1990): 332–45.

Berthrong, Donald J. "Legacies of the Dawes Act: Bureaucrats and Land Thieves at the Cheyenne-Arapahoe Agencies of Oklahoma." In *The American Indian, Past and Present,* edited by Roger L. Nichols. 3d ed. New York: Alfred A. Knopf, 1986.

Blackwood, Evelyn. "Sexuality and Gender in Certain Native American Tribes: The Case of Cross-Culture Females." *Signs* (Autumn 1984): 27–42.

Brenner, Elise M. "To Pray or Be Prey: That is the Question, Strategies for Cultural Autonomy of Massachusetts Praying Town Indians." *Ethnohistory* 27, 2 (1980): 135–52.

Brown, Judith K. "Economic Organization and the Position of Women Among the Iroquois." *Ethnohistory* 17 (Spring 1970): 151–68.

Brumberg, Joan Jacobs. "Zenanas and Girlless Villages: The Ethnology of American Evangelical Women, 1870–1910." *Journal of American History* 69, 2 (1982): 347–71.

Callaway, Donald, Joel Janetski, and Omer C. Stewart. "Ute." In *Great Basin,* edited by Warren L. d'Azevedo. Vol. 11 of *Handbook of North American Indians.* Washington, D.C.: Smithsonian Institution, 1986.

Clemmer, Richard O. "Differential Leadership Patterns In Early Twentieth-Century Great Basin Indian Societies." *Journal of California and Great Basin Anthropology* 11, 1 (1989): 35–49.

Clemmer, Richard O., and Omer C. Stewart. "Treaties, Reservations and Claims." In *Great Basin,* edited by Warren d'Azevedo. Vol. 11 of *Handbook of North American Indians.* Washington, D.C.: Smithsonian Institution, 1986.

Coleman, Michael C. "Not Race, But Grace: Presbyterian Missionary and American Indians, 1873–1893." *Journal of American History* 67 (June 1980): 41–60.

Degler, Carl. "What Ought to Be and What Was: Women's Sexuality in the Nineteenth Century." *American Historical Review* 79 (1974): 479–90.

Eggan, Fred, and Warren d'Azevedo. Introduction to *The Current Status of Anthropological Research in the Great Basin.* Reno, Nev.: Desert Research Institute, 1966.

Emmerich, Lisa. " 'Right in the Midst of My Own People': Native American Women and the Field Matron Program." *American Indian Quarterly* 15 (Summer 1991): 201–16.

Foote, Cheryl J., and Sandra K. Schackel. "Indian Women at New Mexico, 1535–1680." In *New Mexico Women: Intercultural Perspectives,* edited by Joan M. Jensen and Darlis A. Miller. Albuquerque: University of New Mexico Press, 1986.

Fowler, Catherine S. "Subsistence." In *The Current Status of Anthropological Research in the Great Basin,* edited by Warren L. d'Azevedo et al. Reno, Nev.: Desert Research Institute, 1966.

Fowler, Don D. "Great Basin Social Organization." In *Great Basin,* edited by Warren L. d'Azevedo. Vol. 11 of *Handbook of North American Indians.* Washington, D.C.: Smithsonian Institution, 1986.

Fowler, Don D., and David B. Madsen. "Prehistory of the Southeastern Area." In *Great Basin*, edited by Warren L. d'Azevedo. Vol. 11 of *Handbook of North American Indians*. Washington, D.C.: Smithsonian Institution, 1986.

Gray, John S. "The Story of Mrs. Picotte-Galpin, a Sioux Heroine." *Montana* 36 (Summer 1988): 2–21.

Green, Rayna. "The Pocahontas Perplex: The Image of Indian Women in American Culture." *Massachusetts Review* 16, 4 (1975): 698–714.

Goss, James. "Ute Language, Kin, Myth and Nature: A Multidimensional Folk Taxonomy." *Anthropological Linguistics* 9, 9 (1966): 1–11.

——. "Ute Myth as a Cultural Charter." Paper presented at the Great Basin Anthropological Conference, Reno, Nevada, 1990.

Grossberg, Michael. "Who Gets the Child? Custody, Guardianship, and the Rise of a Judicial Patriarchy in Nineteenth-Century America." *Feminist Studies* 9 (Summer 1983): 235–60.

Grumet, Robert Steven. "Sunksquaws, Shamans and Tradeswomen: Middle Atlantic Coastal Algonkian Women During the 17th and 18th Centuries." In *Women and Colonization*, edited by Mona Etienne and Eleanor Leacock. New York: Praeger Publishing, Inc., 1979.

Hagan, William T. "United States Indian Policies, 1860–1900." In *History of Indian-White Relations*, edited by Wilcomb E. Washburn. Vol. 4 of *Handbook of North American Indians*. Washington, D.C.: Smithsonian Institution, 1988.

Harkin, Michael, and Sergei Kan. "Introduction." *Native American Women's Responses to Christianity*, edited by Michael Harkin and Sergei Kan. Special Issue of *Ethnohistory* 42, 3 (1996): 563–69.

Herring, Rebecca J. "The Creation of Indian Farm Women: Field Matrons and Acculturation on the Kiowa-Comanche Reservation, 1895–1906." In *At Home on the Range: Essays on the History of Western Social and Domestic Life*, edited by John R. Wunder. Westport, Conn.: Greenwood Press, 1985.

Holland-Braund, Kathryn E. "Guardians of Tradition and Handmaidens to Change: Women's Roles in Creek Economics and Social Life During the Eighteenth Century." *American Indian Quarterly* 14 (Autumn 1990): 239–58.

Hoxie, Frederick E. "The Curious Story of Reformers and the American Indians." In *Indians in American History*. Arlington Heights, Ill.: Harlan Davidson, Inc., 1988.

Hultkrantz, Ake. "Mythology and Religious Concepts." In *Great Basin*, edited by Warren L. d'Azevedo. Vol. 11 of *Handbook of North American Indians*. Washington, D.C.: Smithsonian Institution, 1986.

Jaimes, M. Annette, and Theresa Halsey. "American Indian Women At the Center of Indigenous Resistance in Contemporary North America." In *The State of Native America*, edited by M. Annette Jaimes. Boston: South End Press, 1992.

Jameson, Elizabeth. "Toward a Multicultural History of Women in the Western United States." *Signs* 13 (Winter 1988): 761–91.

Jorgensen, Joseph G. "Ghost Dance, Bear Dance, Sun Dance." In *Great Basin*, edited by Warren d'Azevedo. Vol. 11 of *Handbook of North American Indians*. Washington, D.C.: Smithsonian Institution, 1986.

Kidwell, Clara Sue. "Indian Women as Cultural Mediators." *Ethnohistory* 39, 2 (1992): 97–107.

———. "The Power of Women in Three Native American Societies." *Journal of Ethnic Studies* 6 (Fall 1978): 113–21.

Klein, Alan M. "The Political-Economy of Gender: A 19th Century Plains Indians Case Study." In *The Hidden Half: Plains Indian Women*, edited by Patricia Albers and Beatrice Medicine. Lanham: University Press of America, 1983.

Klein, Laura F. "Contending with Colonization: Tlinget Men and Women in Change." In *Women and Colonization*, edited by Mona Etienne and Eleanor Leacock. New York: Praeger Publishing, Inc., 1979.

Knack, Martha C. "A Comparative Analysis of Women's Status in Traditional Great Basin Cultures." Typescript in author's possession.

———. "Newspaper Accounts of Indian Women in Southern Nevada Mining Towns, 1870–1900." *Journal of California and Great Basin Anthropology* 8, 1 (1986): 83–98.

———. "Philene T. Hall, Bureau of Indian Affairs Field Matron: Planned Culture Change of Washakie Shoshoni Women." *Prologue: Quarterly of the United States National Archives* 22 (Summer 1990): 150–67.

Kroeber, Alfred L. "Origin Tradition of the Chemehueui Indians." *Journal of American Folklore* 21 (August 1908): 240–42.

———. "Ute Tales." *Journal of American Folklore* 14 (January 1901): 252–83.

Leacock, Eleanor. "Montagnois Women and the Jesuit Program for Colonization." In *Women and Colonization*, edited by Mona Etienne and Eleanor Leacock. New York: Praeger Publishing, Inc., 1979.

Lewis, David Rich. "Reservation Leadership and the Progressive-Traditional Dichotomy: William Wash and the Northern Utes, 1865–1928." *Ethnohistory* 38, 1 (1991): 124–42.

Liberty, Margot. "Hell Came with Horses: Plains Indian Women in the Equestrian Era." *Montana* 32 (Fall 1982): 10–19.

Lowie, Robert A. "Notes on Shoshonean Ethnography." *Anthropology Papers of the American Museum of Natural History* 20, 3 (1924): 185–314.

———. "Shoshonean Tales." *Journal of American Folklore* 37, 143 (1924): 1–91.

Malinowski, Bronislaw. "Dynamics of Culture Change." In *Social Change: The Colonial Situation*, edited by Immanuel Wallerstein. New York: John Wiley and Sons, Inc., 1966.

Malouf, Carling, and John M. Findlay. "Euro-American Impact Before 1870." In *Great Basin*, edited by Warren L. d'Azevedo. Vol. 11 of *Handbook of North American Indians*. Washington, D.C.: Smithsonian Institution, 1986.

Malouf, Carling, and Arlene Malouf. "The Effects of Spanish Slavery on the In-

dians of the Inter-Mountain West." *Southwestern Journal of Anthropology* 1
(1945): 378–91.

Marwitt, John P. "Fremont Culture." In *Great Basin*, edited by Warren L.
d'Azevedo. Vol. 11 of *Handbook of North American Indians*. Washington, D.C.:
Smithsonian Institution, 1986.

Mathes, Valerie Sherer. "Native American Women in Medicine and the Military."
Journal of the West 21 (April 1982): 41–48.

———. "A New Look at the Role of Women in Indian Society." *American Indian
Quarterly* 2 (Summer 1975): 131–39.

McCall, Laura. " 'With All the Wild, Trembling, Rapturous Feelings of a Lover':
Men, Women, and Sexuality in American Literature, 1820–1860." *Journal of
the Early Republic* 14 (Spring 1994): 71–89.

Nelson, Sarah M. "Widowhood and Autonomy in the Native American Southwest." In *On Their Own: Widows and Widowhood in the American Southwest:
1848–1934*, edited by Arlene Scadron. Urbana and Chicago: University of Illinois Press, 1989.

Opler, Marvin K. "The Southern Ute of Colorado." In *Acculturation in Seven
American Indian Tribes*, edited by Ralph Linton. New York: D. Appleton-
Century, 1940.

Pascoe, Peggy. "Western Women at the Cultural Crossroads." In *Trails: Toward a
New Western History*, edited by Patricia Nelson Limerick, Clyde A. Milner III,
and Charles E. Rankin. Lawrence: University Press of Kansas, 1991.

Perdue, Theda. "Cherokee Women and the Trail of Tears." *Journal of Women's
History* 1, 1 (1989): 14–23.

Randle, Martha C. "Iroquois Women, Then and Now." In *Symposium on Local Di-
versity in Iroquois Culture*. Bureau of American Ethnology Bulletin No. 149.
Washington, D.C.: Bureau of American Ethnology, 1951.

Reynolds, Terry R. "Women, Pottery, and Economics of Acoma Pueblo." In *New
Mexico Women: Intercultural Perspectives*, edited by Joan M. Jensen and Darlis
A. Miller. Albuquerque: University of New Mexico Press, 1986.

Richards, Cara. "Matriarchy or Mistake: The Role of Iroquois Women Through
Time." In *Cultural Stability and Culture Change*. Proceedings of the Annual
Meeting of the American Anthropological Society, Seattle, Washington, 1957.

Rothenburg, Diane. "The Mothers of the Nation: Seneca Resistance of Quaker In-
vasion." In *Women and Colonization*, edited by Mona Etienne and Eleanor
Leacock. New York: Praeger Publishing, Inc., 1979.

Sanday, Peggy R. "Female Status in the Public Domain." In *Women, Culture and
Society*, edited by Michelle Zimbalist Rosaldo and Louise Lamphere. Stanford:
Stanford University Press, 1974.

Schlegel, Alice. "Hopi Family Structure and the Experience of Widowhood." In *On
Their Own: Widows and Widowhood in the American Southwest; 1848–1939*, edited
by Arlene Scadron. Urbana and Chicago: University of Illinois Press, 1989.

Schneider, Mary Jane. "Women's Work: An Examination of Women's Roles in Plains Indian Arts and Crafts." In *The Hidden Half: Plains Indian Women*, edited by Patricia Albers and Beatrice Medicine. Lanham: University Press of America, 1983.

Shapiro, Judith. "Kinship." In *Great Basin*, edited by Warren L. d'Azevedo. Vol. 11 of *Handbook of North American Indians*. Washington, D.C.: Smithsonian Institution, 1986.

Shoemaker, Nancy. "The Rise or Fall of Iroquois Women." *Journal of Women's History* 2 (1991): 39–57.

Shimkin, Demetri B. "The Introduction of the Horse." In *Great Basin*, edited by Warren L. d'Azevedo. Vol. 11 of *Handbook of North American Indians*. Washington, D.C.: Smithsonian Institution, 1986.

Smith, Daniel Scott. "Family Limitation, Sexual Control and Domestic Feminism in Victorian America." *Feminist Studies* 1 (Winter–Spring 1973): 40–57.

Smith, Michael T. "The History of Indian Citizenship." In *The American, Indian Past and Present*, edited by Roger L. Nichols. 3d ed. New York: Alfred A. Knopf, 1986.

Smith, Sherry L. "Beyond Princess and Squaw: Army Officers Perceptions of Indian Women." In *The Woman's West*, edited by Susan Armitage and Elizabeth Jameson. Norman: University of Oklahoma Press, 1987.

Smits, David D. "The 'Squaw Drudge': A Prime Index of Savagism." *Ethnohistory* 29, 4 (1982): 218–306.

Social Science Research Council. "Acculturation: An Explanatory Formulation." In *Beyond the Frontier*, edited by Paul Bohannan and Fred Plog. Garden City, N.J.: Natural History Press, 1967.

Spicer, Edward H. "Spanish-Indian Acculturation in the Southwest." *American Anthropologist* 56 (1954): 661–84.

———. "Types of Contact and Processes of Change." In *Perspectives in American Indian Culture Change*. Chicago: University of Chicago Press, 1961.

Spindler, Louise, and George Spindler. "Male and Female Adaptations to Culture Change." *American Anthropologist* 60 (April 1958): 217–33.

Stearns, Carol Z., and Peter N. Stearns. "Victorian Sexuality: Can Historians Do It Better?" *Journal of Social History* 18 (1984–85): 626–33.

Stewart, Omer C. "Culture Element Distributions XVIII — Ute, Southern Paiute." *University of California Anthropology Records* 6, 4 (1942): 231–356.

———. "The Peyote Religion." In *Great Basin*, edited by Warren L. d'Azevedo. Vol. 11 of *Handbook of North American Indians*. Washington, D.C.: Smithsonian Institution, 1986.

———. "Southern Ute Adjustment to Modern Living." In *Acculturation in the Americas*, edited by Sol Tax. Chicago: University of Chicago Press, 1952.

Szasz, Margaret Connell. " 'Poor Richard' Meets the Native American: Schooling for Young Indian Women in Early Eighteenth Century Connecticut." *Pacific Historical Review* 49, 2 (1980): 215–35.

Trennert, Robert A. "Educating Indian Girls at Nonreservation Boarding Schools, 1878–1920." In *The American Indian, Past and Present*, edited by Roger L. Nichols. 3d ed. New York: Alfred A. Knopf, 1986.

——. "From Carlisle to Phoenix: The Rise and Fall of the Indian Outing System, 1878–1930." *Pacific Historical Review* 52 (August 1983): 267–92.

Tyler, S. Lyman. "The Spaniard and the Ute." *Utah Historical Quarterly* 22 (Winter 1954): 343–61.

——. "The Yuta Indians Before 1880." *Western Humanities Review* 5 (Spring 1951): 153–63.

Walkowitz, Daniel J. "The Making of a Feminine Professional Identity: Social Workers in the 1900s." *American Historical Review* 95 (October 1980): 1051–75.

Weist, Katherine M. "Plains Indian Women: An Assessment." In *Anthropology on the Great Plains*, edited by W. Raymond Wood and Margot Liberty. Lincoln: University of Nebraska Press, 1980.

Welter, Barbara. "The Cult of True Womanhood: 1800–1860." *American Quarterly* 18, 4 (166): 151–74.

——. "The Feminization of American Religion: 1800–1860." In *Clio's Consciousness Raised*, edited by Mary S. Hartman and Lois Banner. New York: Harper & Row Publishers, 1974.

——. " 'She Hath Done What She Could': Protestant Women's Missionary Careers in Nineteenth-Century America." *American Quarterly* (Winter 1978): 624–38.

Wilson, Terry P. "Osage Indian Women During a Century of Change, 1870–1980." *Prologue* 14 (Winter 1982): 185–202.

THESES AND DISSERTATIONS

Emmerich, Lisa. " 'To Respect and Love and Seek the Ways of White Women': Field Matrons, The Office of Indian Affairs, and Civilization Policy, 1890–1928." Ph.D. diss., University of Maryland, 1987.

Hoyt, Milton. "The Development of Education Among the Southern Utes." Ph.D. diss., University of Colorado, Boulder, 1967.

Johnson, Charles Clark. "A Study of Modern Southwestern Indian Leadership." Ph.D. diss., University of Colorado, Boulder, 1963.

McKee, Elizabeth A. "Civilizing the Indian: Field Matrons Under Hoopa Valley Agency Jurisdiction 1898–1919." Master's thesis, California State University, 1982.

Osburn, Katherine M. B. " 'And as the Squaws Are a Secondary Consideration': Southern Ute Women Under Directed Culture Change, 1887–1934." Ph.D. diss., University of Denver, 1993.

Satersmoen, Carol. "Cultural Change Among the Northern and Southern Utes as Represented by the Beadwork Collections of the Colorado Historical Society." Unpublished master's paper, Department of Anthropology Library, University of Denver, Denver, Colorado, 1990.

Swadesh, Frances Leon. "The Southern Utes and Their Neighbors, 1877–1926." Master's thesis, University of Colorado, 1962.

Wanken, Helen M. " 'Women's Sphere' and Indian Reform: The Woman's National Indian Association, 1879–1901." Ph.D. diss., Marquette University, 1981.

Index